MAN-MONKEY

"AS DOES COME, EVER SINCE THE MAN DROWNED IN THE CUT"

NICK REDFERN

IN SEARCH OF THE BRITISH BIGFOOT

Typeset Edited by Jonathan Downes
Cover design and Layout by Mark North for CFZ Communications
Using Microsoft Word 2000, Microsoft , Publisher 2000, Adobe Photoshop CS.

First published in Great Britain by CFZ Press 2007

**CFZ Press
Myrtle Cottage
Woolsery
Bideford
North Devon
EX39 5QR**

© CFZ MMVII

All rights reserved. Without limiting the rights under copyright reserved above, no part of this publication may be reproduced, stored in or introduced into a re-trieval system, or transmitted, in any form of by any means (electronic, mechani-cal, photocopying, recording or otherwise), without the prior written permission of both the copyright owners and the publishers of this book.

ISBN: 978-1-905723-16-4

'A very weird story of an encounter with an animal ghost arose of late years within my knowledge. On the 21st of January 1879, a labouring man was employed to take a cart of luggage from Ranton in Staffordshire to Woodcock, beyond Newport in Shropshire, for the ease of a party of visitors who were going from one house to another. He was late in coming back; his horse was tired, and could only crawl along at a foot's pace, so that it was ten o'clock at night when he arrived at the place where the highroad crosses the Birmingham and Liverpool Canal.

'Just before he reached the canal bridge, a strange black creature with great white eyes sprang out of the plantation by the roadside and alighted on his horse's back. He tried to push it off with his whip, but to his horror the whip went through the thing, and he dropped it on the ground in fright.

'The poor, tired horse broke into a canter, and rushed onwards at full speed with the ghost still clinging to its back. How the creature at length vanished, the man hardly knew. He told his tale in the village of Woodseaves, a mile further on, and so effectively frightened the hearers that one man actually stayed with friends there all night, rather than cross the terrible bridge which lay between him and his home.'

From *Shropshire Folklore* by Charlotte S. Burne
and Georgina F. Jackson, 1883

Books by Nick Redfern:

A Covert Agenda
The FBI Files
Cosmic Crashes
Strange Secrets (with Andy Roberts)
Three Men Seeking Monsters
Body Snatchers in the Desert
On the Trail of the Saucer Spies
Celebrity Secrets
Man Monkey - In Search of the British Bigfoot
Memoirs of a Monster Hunter

CONTENTS

Introduction 7

Chapter I: 'The Terrible Bridge' 9

Chapter II: An Unearthly Child 17

Chapter III: The Quest Begins 23

Chapter IV: The Shugborough Affair 31

Chapter V: Walking the Woods 37

Chapter VI: The Cult of the Moon-Beast 45

Chapter VII: The Encounters Continue 57

Chapter VIII: Disaster at the Bridge 65

Chapter IX: A Close Encounter of the Hairy Kind 85

Chapter X: The Monkey and the Serpent 91

Chapter XI: The Horn Dance 99

Chapter XII: The Man-Monkey Returns 107

Chapter XIII: Who Goes There? 113

Chapter XIV: The Hairy Hands and Other Things 117

Chapter XV: On the Trail of the Kelpie 127

Chapter XVI: Black Dog Parallels 131

Conclusions 139

Acknowledgments 141

Chronology of Events 143

References 145

INTRODUCTION

For the most part, the dark and convoluted story that follows covers the period from 1986 to early 2001, and is, for me at least, a time that I look back on with a high degree of both nostalgia and fondness. Moreover, aside from a very few, and relatively minor, excursions of the strictly UFOlogical kind, it represents a specific period in my life that I have seldom chronicled in book form before. And it was the action of finally doing so at length that brought back a lot of memories – the good, the bad, the ugly and the undoubtedly mad. But perhaps most important of all, it was the very act of digging through all of my old note-books, audio-tapes and photographs, and actually (and finally) getting around to writing the damned thing that made me realise what a strange, surreal and macabre saga that of the diabolical Man-Monkey really was and - for those, at least, whose lives were adversely affected by their personal encounters with the mysterious beast - still is.

It is highly unlikely that this book will come to represent the final word on the creature that is known as the Man-Monkey; and nor should it either. Indeed, the pages that follow merely represent my own personal discoveries, thoughts, observations and conclusions that were generated during that long-gone period in which my studies and enquiries occurred. Doubtless as time progresses more data, additional witness testimony, and new material evidence will continue to surface into the cryptozoological community, as it always seems to do in weird little affairs such as this.

And if that does indeed happen, I sincerely hope that it will encourage some other enterprising researcher and/or writer to pick up at the point where I left off some six years ago. Or, quite possibly, it may even prompt me to once again plunge head-long into those darkened, shadowy woods that are home to the hairy man-beast that has for so long both intrigued and obsessed me – and in equal, heady measures. The future, however, is not what concerns us at this particular moment in time. No: it is upon a strange and surreal journey into England's most mysterious and dark past that we must now well and truly embark.

CHAPTER I
'THE TERRIBLE BRIDGE'

Constructed in the early part of the 19th Century, England's historic Shropshire Union Canal, or the 'Shroppie' - as it has come to be affectionately and popularly known by those that regularly travel its extensive and winding waters – is some sixty-seven miles in length and extends from Ellesmere Port near the city of Liverpool right down to Autherley Junction at Wolverhampton in the Midlands. The southern end of the canal, that was originally known as the Birmingham and Liverpool Junction Canal, was the very last of the great British narrow-boat canals to be built; and is a true testament to the masterful engineering of Thomas Telford. Deep cuttings and massive embankments are the veritable hallmarks of the canal and they paint a picture that is as eerie as it is picturesque.

Not only that: the Shropshire Union Canal is quite possibly Britain's most haunted waterway; as the local folk that intimately know and appreciate the history and lore of the canal are only too well aware. At Chester's old Northgate, for example, and where the canal was dug into part of the town's old moat, a ghostly Roman centurion can be seen – when circumstances are said to be right – still guarding the ancient entrance to the city. Then there is the 'shrieking spectre' of Belton Cutting: a veritable wailing, Banshee-style monstrosity that strikes cold fear into the hearts of those who have the misfortune and bad luck to cross its path.

At the site of the former lock-keeper's cottage at Burgedin, on the nearby Montgomery Canal, come intriguing reports of the ghostly figure of an early Welsh princess named Eira. And bringing matters relatively more up to date, there is the spectral American Air Force pilot whose aircraft crashed near the canal at Little Onn, at Church Eaton, Staffordshire during the Second World War; and the 'helpful resident ghost' of Tyrley Middle Lock at Market Drayton, which has allegedly been seen opening and closing the lock-gates for those novice boaters that from time to time negotiate the waters of the long canal.

But by far the most famous – or perhaps infamous would be more accurate – ghostly resident of the Shropshire Union Canal is a truly diabolical and devilish entity that has become known as the Man-Monkey. It was within the packed pages of Charlotte Sophia Burne's book of 1883, *Shropshire Folklore* that the unholy antics of what some have since perceived to be the closest thing that Britain may have to the North American Bigfoot and the Yeti of the Himalayas, were first unleashed upon an unsuspecting general public. According to Burne:

'A very weird story of an encounter with an animal ghost arose of late years within my knowledge. On the 21st of January 1879, a labouring man was employed to take a cart of luggage from Ranton in Staffordshire to Woodcock, beyond Newport in Shropshire, for the ease of a party of visitors who were going from one house to another. He was late in coming back; his horse was tired, and could only crawl along at a foot's pace, so that it was ten o'clock at night when he arrived at the place where the highroad crosses the Birmingham and Liverpool Canal.'

It was then, Burne faithfully recorded, that the man received what was undoubtedly the most terrifying shock of his entire life – before or since, it seems safe to assume: 'Just before he reached the canal bridge, a strange black creature with great white eyes sprang out of the plantation by the roadside and alighted on his horse's back. He tried to push it off with his whip, but to his horror the whip went through the thing, and he dropped it on the ground in fright.'

Needless to say, Burne added: 'The poor, tired horse broke into a canter, and rushed onwards at full speed with the ghost still clinging to its back. How the creature at length vanished, the man hardly knew.' But the story was far from over, Burne learned: 'He told his tale in the village of Woodseaves, a mile further on, and so effectively frightened the hearers that one man actually stayed with friends there all night, rather than cross the terrible bridge which lay between him and his home.'

Burne's wild story continued that, by the time he reached the village of Woodseaves the un-named man was in a state of 'excessive terror'

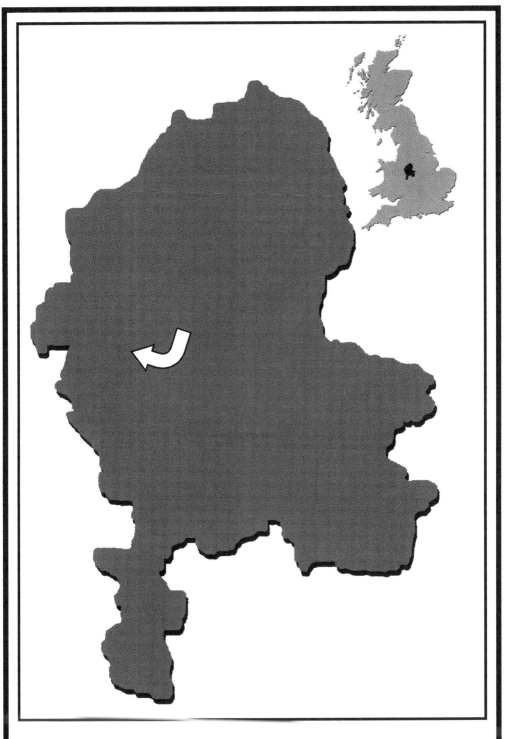

Staffordshire, showing the position of the Man-Monkey's haunt with reference to the rest of the county.

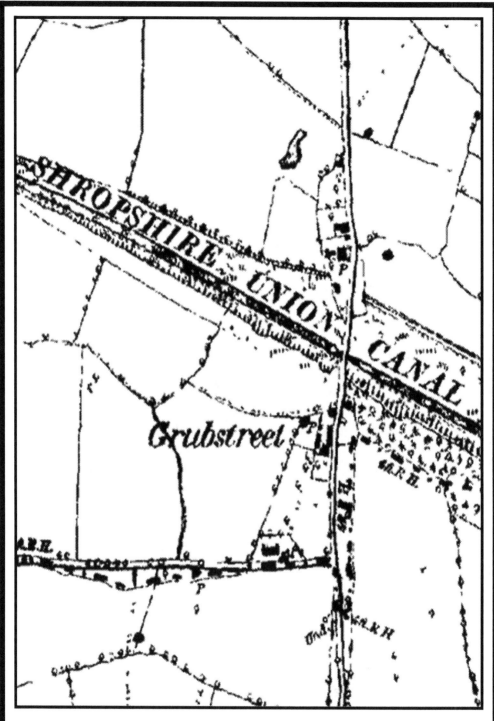

Bridge 39 over the canal - from an 1891 map (only twelve years after the first `Man-Monkey` encounter..)

and promptly retired to his bed for several days 'so much was he prostrated by his fright'. Burne also recorded that on the following day, another individual travelled back to the sinister bridge and, sure enough, there was the man's whip, still lying at the very place where it had fallen to the ground after the nightmarish and bizarre encounter.

Perhaps inevitably, dark tales of the crazed beast and its infernal night-time activities began to spread like absolute wildfire throughout the little villages and hamlets of the area, as Burne quickly learned and recorded thus in her book: 'The adventure, as was natural, was much talked of in the neighbourhood, and, of course, with all sorts of variations.'

But, it seems that the local constabulary had heard all about the nature and exploits of the hairy demon and knew exactly what was afoot, as Burne carefully chronicled: 'Some days later the man's master was surprised by a visit from a policeman, who came to request him to give information of his having been stopped and robbed on the Big Bridge on the night of the 21st January.'

The 'master', apparently much amused by this development in the story, carefully explained to the visiting policeman that this was completely untrue; and that, in reality, it was his employee who had reported a strange encounter at the 'Big Bridge', but that there was most definitely no robbery involved at all. Interestingly, when the *real* details of what had occurred were related to the policeman, he was seemingly completely nonplussed and merely replied in a distinctly matter-of-fact fashion: 'Oh, was that all, sir? Oh, I know what that was. That was the Man-Monkey, sir, as does come again at that bridge ever since the man was drowned in the cut.'

Charlotte Burne also revealed that she personally had the opportunity to speak with the man's employer herself, but she did not elaborate upon the specific nature of the conversation within the pages of *Shropshire Folklore*. Nevertheless, Burne did describe the master as being a 'Mr. B_____ of L_____d'. And although the man's name remains unknown to us, 'L_____d' is very possibly a reference to the ancient Staffordshire city of Lichfield.

So what, precisely, was the strange, hairy critter that was seen wildly

SHROPSHIRE FOLK-LORE:

A Sheaf of Gleanings.

EDITED BY

CHARLOTTE SOPHIA BURNE

FROM THE COLLECTIONS OF

GEORGINA F. JACKSON.

'The history of no people can be said to have been written so long as its superstitions and beliefs in past times have not been studied.'—*Professor Rhys.*

London:
TRÜBNER & CO., 57 & 59, LUDGATE HILL.
SHREWSBURY: ADNITT & NAUNTON.
CHESTER: MINSHULL & HUGHES.
1883.

[*All Rights reserved.*]

crosses the Birmingham and Liverpool Canal. Just before he reached
the canal bridge, a strange black creature with great white eyes sprang
out of the plantation by the road-side and alighted on his horse's
back. He tried to push it off with his whip, but to his horror the
whip went *through* the Thing, and he dropped it to the ground in his
fright. The poor tired horse broke into a canter, and rushed onwards
at full speed with the ghost still clinging to its back. How the
creature at length vanished the man hardly knew. He told his tale
in the village of Woodseaves, a mile further on, and so effectually
frightened the hearers that one man actually stayed with his friends
there all night, rather than cross the terrible bridge which lay between
him and his home. The ghost-seer reached home at length, still in
a state of excessive terror (but, as his master assured me, perfectly
sober), and it was some days before he was able to leave his bed, so
much was he prostrated by his fright. The whip was searched for
next day, and found just at the place where he said he had dropped it.

Now comes the curious part of the story. The adventure, as
was natural, was much talked of in the neighbourhood, and of course
with all sorts of variations. Some days later the man's master (Mr.
B—— of L——d) was surprised by a visit from a policeman, who
came to request him to give information of his having been stopped
and robbed on the Big Bridge on the night of the 21st January!
Mr. B——, much amused, denied having been robbed, either on the
canal bridge or anywhere else, and told the policeman the story just
related. 'Oh, was that all, sir?' said the disappointed policeman.
'Oh, I know what *that* was. That was the Man-Monkey, sir, as *does*
come again at that bridge ever since the man was drowned in the
Cut!'[1]

I heard this from Mr. B—— himself, a week or two later.

Let us now cross the county, from north-east to south-west.
'The Roarin' Bull o' Bagbury,' although he has been 'laid' for
generations, is still talked of about Bishop's Castle and all along the
Shropshire side of the Border. Hyssington, the scene of his conquest
by the assembled parsons, is a parish partly in Shropshire and partly
in Montgomeryshire, which here runs up into Shropshire in a penin-

[1] Cut = canal. See *Shropshire Word-Book.*

roaming the distinctly darkened corners of the Shropshire Union Canal by moonlight on that winter's night way back in January 1879? Was it truly some form of Bigfoot or Yeti-like entity? Could it potentially have been an exotic escapee of the simian kind, and possibly one that originated with a private zoo somewhere in the area? Did it have wholly supernatural and paranormal origins rather than purely physical ones? Or was it something else entirely? These, and many others too, are the probing and problematic questions that have fascinated me for years – almost, I freely admit, to the point of complete and utter obsession.

For a very long while, it has been my firm intention to relate in print the facts pertaining to that strange period (from early 1986 to early 2001) which saw me immersed, to varying degrees, in the bizarre saga of the Man-Monkey. Unfortunately, for many a year I was tied up with a multitude of other writing-based projects; and, as a direct result, there simply were not enough hours in the day to do the complex story the full justice that it most certainly required and chronicle it in its entirety. That said, however, I now have a little more breathing space at my disposal; and so, as the mighty *Sex Pistols* so correctly and concisely put it back in the long-gone days of 1978: 'The time is right to do it now.'

CHAPTER II
AN UNEARTHLY CHILD

My deep fascination with strange and bizarre creatures extends well back into my early childhood; and specifically to a key event that I can still vaguely recall to this very day. It was (as Brian Adams once put it in his less-than-classic song of the same name) the summer of '69, and I was just four years of age. My parents had taken me to Scotland for a week's holiday and we were staying in a pleasant hotel situated in the picturesque town of Oban. I have three, and indeed *only* three, brief and fragmentary memories of that particular week: one was of my father almost hitting an irate driver (twice!) as we negotiated the busy roads of Glasgow on the north-bound journey from our then-home in Staffordshire. The second was of someone reversing into my parents' *Hillman Imp* car in Oban and causing damage to the rear-bumper. And the third was an exciting trip to what is surely that most mysterious and monstrous of all locales: the always-atmospheric Loch Ness.

I can still just about remember happily playing on the shores of the huge loch and listening intently as my father had a deep discussion about the Loch Ness Monster with an elderly couple that had driven there in an old camper-style vehicle; with the specific intent of seeking out for themselves the diabolical and monstrous beast that was said to lurk within the loch's deep, dark, peat-soaked waters. I was well and truly wide-eyed with wonder and awe when I heard that there was very possibly a still-living dinosaur thriving deep within its sinister depths. And, from that specific moment onwards, my life was forever changed.

Practically from the time that I could read, I would heartily devour just about anything and everything on the strange and twilight world of the unknown that I could get my eager hands on. Even as a seven-year-old, my heaving book shelves were literally crammed to bursting point with complete collections of *The Secret Seven*; *The Famous Five*; C.S. Lewis's tales of Narnia; and all-things of a similar, fantasy and adventure-driven nature. But, those same shelves were also full of titles on werewolves, vampires, the Yeti, Bigfoot, lake-monsters, witches, warlocks and wizards.

Night after night, I would bury my head deep under the sheets with my trusty torch in one hand and a well-thumbed copy of one of my prized and precious books in the other – both wide-eyed and amazed at the startling accounts of the weird, wonderful and monstrous things that were said to secretly live among us. Just occasionally, when dark thoughts of fantastic creatures would practically over-whelm my young and impressionable mind, I would dare to lift my head from under those same sheets and stare intently into the dark-ened corners of my old oak wardrobe, the door of which always seemed to be slightly – and suspiciously - ajar. As children all across the world have done for years (and no doubt will continue to do so for years to come), I would scare myself stupid wondering if some-thing ancient and unholy really *did* lurk deep within the dark and shadowy recesses of that old wardrobe. But, if it did, it summarily failed to ever show itself to me.

For the next few years my interest in all things odd, macabre, and ad-venturous never really wavered even once; and I would always look forward to the school holidays – and particularly those glorious, seemingly-never-ending six weeks of summer when teachers, les-sons, and home-work were summarily forgotten about by millions of children all across the green and pleasant land that is Great Britain – and when me and my friends, Chuck, Tim, Jeremy, and Dave, would furiously ride our pedal-bikes around the woods, fields, and com-mons of the village of Pelsall, where I lived as a kid.

Although we always liked to think of ourselves as the slightly oik-ish, West Midlands-equivalents of the aforementioned *Famous Five* and *Secret Seven*, we never did find any buried treasure, capture any dastardly smugglers, or have a celebratory feast of cake and lemon-ade with the Lord-Mayor of Walsall for helping the local plod to solve some dark and fiendish plot. But we did at least *try* to play the part if nothing else; and thoughts of strange beasts and adventurous romps were never far from my imaginative mind, on those summery days and nights of the early-to-mid 1970s, as the Gang-of-Five roamed Pelsall's remote North Common. And for those of you that think the West Midlands is nothing but a bleak industrial, concrete nightmare, the North Common is actually a surprisingly large and atmospheric location, that could easily double for the wilds of Dartmoor – and particularly so on a suitably dark and stormy, windswept night.

But then, at the age of eleven, in the winter of 1976, things changed dramatically for me and the memorable creations of Enid Blyton, Bram Stoker, Mary Shelley and C.S. Lewis were quickly and firmly replaced by girls, the vitriolic tones of Johnny Rotten, and the earsplitting major-chords of guitar-thug-supremo, Steve Jones. Yes: punk rock, the *Sex Pistols*, and puberty had all well and truly arrived like a bolt from the blue; and the Loch Ness Monster and its strange ilk were utterly gone.

In the immediate years that followed, my life was like that of most typical young, suburban teenagers living in late 1970s central England, and it progressed very nicely to a soundtrack that was dominated by the hallowed tones of (among numerous others) *The Skids, The Vapors, The Only Ones, The Undertones, The Buzzcocks,* and *The Jam.* Teenage parties, spiky hair (yes, even *I* had hair back then – spiky, too!), skinny black ties, copious amounts of Strongbow, Woodpecker, and snake-bite, spin-the-bottle, and drunken sing-alongs to the *Sex Pistols'* 'Friggin' in the Riggin'` were the order of the day. In fact, I have to say that in 2007, the spiky hair aside, not a lot has really changed!

By the time that we all reached the age of seventeen, the local pubs, *The Swan,* and *The George & Dragon,* were the Friday and Saturday night places to hang out for me and my friends as we got merrily drunk, and set out to try and pick up the female population of Pelsall. And sometimes it worked, and sometimes it didn't. Then, from around 1982 to the summer of 1985, me, Dave, another Dave, and a friend named Ian, rented a large caravan in the Devonshire town of Brixham, and one that was a true home from home, and where we had a lot of chaotic and uproarious fun. It was during this particular time period that I undertook a year-long stint as a writer working on a music, fashion and entertainment magazine that went by the moniker of *Zero* - and which was truly one of the happiest times in my life. I most certainly can't say that it was *exactly* akin to Hunter S. Thompson's classic tale *The Rum Diary;* but I do like to think that it was pretty close.

By the end of 1985, however, the job with *Zero* was gone, and it had become graphically and depressingly clear to me that I was now in dire need of money. The real world was unfortunately beckoning and I was very nearly skint. And, so, I was soon back in Walsall and working full-time as a van-driver for a company that sold paint and wallpaper. Of the very few 9-to-5 jobs I have ever had in my life, I didn't really mind this one too much, as I was out of the boss's hair, driving around, making deliveries to the painters and decorators of Staffordshire and the West Midlands, and all to the hallowed sound-track of Radio 1 that would relentlessly blare out of the van's speakers throughout the entire day. Aside, that is, from whenever Simon Bates insisted on utterly torturing the airwaves, if not the entire British nation, with the utterly sickening and always-doom-laden *Our Tune*, during which I would regularly and quickly hit the 'Off' button.

Practically every day, my long and winding route would take me to the large and sprawling forest known as the Cannock Chase, from which at the time in question I lived only about four miles. A high plateau bordered by the Trent Valley to the north, and the West Midlands to the south, the huge and picturesque Chase has been an integral feature of the Staffordshire landscape for generations. Following an initial invasion of Britain in A.D. 43, Roman forces advanced to the south to what is now the town of Cannock and along a route that would become known as Watling Street, a major, and historic, Roman road. The surrounding countryside was very heavily wooded even back then, as can be demonstrated by the Romans' name for the area: *Letocetum*, or the Grey Woods.

While out driving across the Chase, and soaking in the glorious majesty of those huge and mighty trees, my mind would often wander back with much affection to those long-gone days and nights as a monster-obsessed child; and, perhaps inevitably, to those exciting stories of the strange creatures that were said to inhabit the thick woods there. Indeed, even way back in the mid-1970s, as I very well knew, seemingly magical tales were quietly told by the local folk of the area; sightings of big-cats, wild boar, and even the occasional wallaby on the loose deep within the dense, expansive forest.

And it was around this particular time that my interest in all-things-weird slowly started to resurface. As a direct result, I duly began to subscribe to some of the self-published newsletters on UFOs that existed at the time – such as the then-photocopied, fanzine-style periodical of Graham and Mark Birdsall's *Yorkshire UFO Society*, which would prove to be a *very* early precursor to their glossy, newsstand *UFO Magazine* of the 1990s. I also succeeded in finding *Reader's World* - a great little shop tucked away in a Birmingham side-street, that was a veritable treasure-trove for out-of-print and hard-to-find books on just about all aspects of the paranormal, the mysterious, and the conspiratorial.

It was not too long afterwards that my path first crossed with that of the infamous Man-Monkey of the Shropshire Union Canal. And it is a day that I will always remember, for one, central reason. Although somewhat appropriately for what was most certainly such a diabolical beast, it was not a good reason: not at all. From a book-seller whose name and location have now well and truly been long lost to the inevitable fog of time, I had ordered a cheap, used copy of Janet and Colin Bord's book *Alien Animals* – a classic and essential title that dug deep into the many world-wide legends and tales of ghostly black dogs, mysterious big cats, hairy man-beasts, winged monstrosities, and those unknown denizens of the deep, such as the Loch Ness Monster, Ogopogo, as well as a multitude of sea-serpents.

It was in January 1986, I very well recall, when *Alien Animals* finally arrived in the mail. I eagerly sat down to read it, and was completely amazed to find mention of the infamous Man-Monkey; a creature that I had never previously come across, but that the Bords said haunted the canals and the woods of an area that, as it so transpired, was actually only a short drive by car from my then-rooms. However, my first exposure to the Man-Monkey was firmly overshadowed by a far more ominous event that had occurred on the same day that I had begun to read the book: the tragic and fatal explosion in the United States of the Space Shuttle *Challenger.*

I continued to heartily devour *Alien Animals* and made a careful, mental note to make the drive out to the infamous bridge where the Man-Monkey was said to have its lair. However, beer, girls, and work were the order of the day, and even though my interest in the world of the unexplained had been well and truly rejuvenated by now, and certainly to levels that easily exceeded those of my earlier, childhood years, I simply forgot about the Man-Monkey and began to focus my attention more on unidentified flying objects – that is, until the latter part of 1987.

It was during this specific period in time that I was working down in the Essex town of Harlow. The company that was then employing me was paying for a very nice hotel room, and I most certainly had no complaints at all: there was a wealth of fine and delicious food, the plentiful supply of booze ran flowingly, and there was a more than adequate night-life in town, and one that was replete with a regular supply of white-stiletto-wearing Essex Girls.

One evening, in October 1987, I was sprawled out on the bed, triple-whisky-and-coke in hand (or some such similar potent concoction, at least), and once again thumbing through the pages of *Alien Animals* – probably, I'm pretty sure, for the very first time since that fateful day back in January 1986. Oddly, this occasion, too, would be hit by deep tragedy: namely, the devastating hurricane that decimated whole swathes of England, after BBC weather-man Michael Fish had earnestly assured the good folk of Britain that any talk of a coming hurricane was complete and utter nonsense. Fish was wrong, of course; memorably so, in fact, as the nation found out to its considerable cost when it arose to an apocalyptic scene of complete and utter carnage the next day.

I actually recall waking up in the early hours, with macabre images of the Man-Monkey fixed firmly in my mind, as well as hearing the driving deluge, and the wild storm whipping up a veritable frenzy outside of the rain-beaten windows. Later, like so many others, I strongly suspect, I drove around much of Essex, amazed and appalled, yet also spell-bound and transfixed at the scene of overwhelming destruction and carnage that the mighty storm had wrought upon Britain's much beloved countryside overnight. It may have been nothing but mere coincidence and imagination, of course, yet it seemed to me in those slightly paranoid and dark moments which occasionally surfaced that whenever I chose to delve into the macabre world of the Man-Monkey, disaster seemed to quickly and inevitably follow.

CHAPTER III
THE QUEST BEGINS

Although, as I have related, my interest in the tale of the Man-Monkey dated back to 1986, it was not really until 1989 that I actively became involved in an investigation of the hairy monstrosity in any real and meaningful capacity. And somewhat appropriately, even the beginnings of that research were shrouded in surreal synchronicity and distinct high-strangeness. It was in that same year that my fraught and fractured relationship to the tiring and stressed-out world of 9 to 5 finally came to a complete and crashing end, when I took the plunge and quit my job, pooled my meagre savings, and well and truly embarked upon the career of a freelance writer.

Approximately three months or so before I left the wretched real-world behind me, however, and during which time I was once again working as a van-driver for the same aforementioned paint-and-wallpaper company, I began to make regular deliveries to the residence of a Rugeley, Staffordshire painter-and-decorator named Graham Allen. As there was never anyone at home when I made my drops, I would simply leave the order, along with the receipt of purchase. I did not know it at the time, but Graham had an intense interest in all things UFOlogical and mysterious, and he was a veritable fountain of knowledge on the attendant mysteries and the ancient folklore of the Cannock Chase. Indeed, this would not become apparent to me until 1996, some seven years later, when I finally met Graham in person at the first-anniversary conference of the Staffordshire UFO Group, of which he was vice-president and second-in-command to SUFOG founder, Irene Bott.

On one fateful occasion, at the height of the summer of 1989, and just as I was about to climb into the cab of my van and depart from Graham's pleasant residence, a loud yet squeaky voice over my shoulder shouted something akin to: 'Hold on, pal.' I turned around to see a distinctly strange looking character hovering suspiciously behind me. It was a man of short height, and of scrawny – even emaciated, I would say - build. He was, I estimated, in his mid-forties, and had thick, black greasy hair that was raked across his head. He wore a pair of bottle-top glasses, and had about five days worth of grey-black stubble. He was dressed in a dirty black suit, a *Motorhead* t-shirt, battered white trainers, and stunk to high-heaven of what smelt suspiciously like fox piss. He reminded me of a younger - and even seedier - version of Albert Steptoe.

'Do you sell to the public?' he asked me. 'I'm decorating.'

'Well, yeah, but you'll have to come to the shop; it's in Walsall, up in the Birchills,' I replied, in reference to the area of the town that was home to my place of employment.

'Cracking,' was the man's single word, and he promptly strolled away, whistling. As I would come to learn in the weeks ahead, 'cracking' was quite possibly his favourite word. Needless to say, I quickly and totally forgot about the odd chap until he walked into the shop just a few, short days later, while I was sat atop a fork-lift truck, and deeply engaged in unloading a huge pallet of paint that was positioned on a large lorry outside of the back doors.

'Ho, there!' he shouted from the other end of the building. 'Remember me?' I did not. At least, that is I didn't until I had fin-ished my unloading and headed up to the counter to serve him. 'I'm from Rugeley,' was his odd, and only, introduction, I still vaguely recall to this day. I nodded both aimlessly and unenthusiastically.

'I need paint,' he said, succinctly. Nearly twenty years on, I can still remember that it had been a hell of a day for some reason, and I was certainly in no mood at all for his annoying and utter vagueness. So, I said to him by way of a reply that we had lots of paint, in lots of cans, and in lots of colours and in lots of sizes too; and so, therefore, could he be just a tad more specific? Completely ignoring my ques-tions, however, he merely said: 'My name's Fletcher.' Once again, and still totally bored, I nodded, caring not in the slightest what the hell this eccentric character's name was or indeed was not. Anyway, after about five minutes of listening to his completely aimless ram-blings, I finally got his order taken care of; however, as the rain was absolutely bucketing down outside, and as Fletcher was faced with a ten or fifteen minute walk back to Walsall's main bus-station in the centre of town, he hung around the shop for a while, as I prepared my delivery-list for the following morning.

'Deliver every day to the Cannock Chase, do you?' he asked, seemingly innocently.

'Yeah, usually,' I replied, still completely unmoved by his odd small talk.

'Some very weird shit happens over there, you know,' he added. Now *that* at least got my attention. I stopped what I was doing, leaned on the counter, told him of my deep interest in both UFOlogy and cryptozoology, and asked him to explain to me precisely what he meant.

'Make me a cuppa and I'll tell you,' he said, enigmatically and with a disturbing, shifty smile on his gaunt, stubbly visage. And so, for the next twenty minutes or so, and as we both sat on the aforementioned pallet of paint drinking mugs of hot, sweet, milky tea, Fletcher began to open up and talk. However, as I only got the very barest of bones of his strange tale due to the grand responsibilities of the worlds of wallpaper and paint, a meeting was duly arranged: we were set to rendezvous at a Rugeley café on the following Saturday afternoon.

I drove over there on the day in question, not really knowing what to expect at all and sat on a bench outside, awaiting Fletcher's imminent arrival. At said meeting, and as we took our seats on what was a depressing, grey, downcast day, it became quickly obvious to me that Fletcher was deeply troubled at an emotional level, and was highly unpleasant, too. Although I had no absolutely idea what it was called at the time, he was overwhelmingly afflicted by what today would be considered a classic case of Obsessive-Compulsive Disorder. I noted with fascination and much cruel hilarity how, every time he would take a bite to eat, he would immediately thereafter tap his right fore-finger softly on the table, after which he would cough precisely twice. After about five minutes of watching this very weird character at work, I asked Fletcher outright why he did this. He quietly replied something along the lines of: 'If I don't do it, things will start to go wrong.'

It is most certainly not my wish to label obsessive-compulsives unfairly; but Fletcher was, to put it bluntly, a veritable loon of the absolute highest order. Not only that, and somewhat puzzlingly, I was never able to get Fletcher to reveal to me if that was his first name or his last name. But everyone in the café seemed to know him by that sole moniker. Indeed, as we entered its steamy and smoky confines, the utterly bored Brummy waitress behind the counter greeted him with but two words: 'Alright, Fletch?' He nodded in her direction in a decidedly grim fashion.

As I said, as well as being utterly deranged and damaged, Fletcher was deeply unpleasant, too: he had an overwhelming obsession with tales of allegedly-real snuff films, as well as victims of fatal car accidents. Indeed, he related proudly to me how he had a contact – or *claimed* to have a contact, would perhaps be a far more accurate description - in the Staffordshire emergency services, who had secretly supplied him with a batch of grisly pictures of several dead and pummeled bodies pulled from the carnage of a multiple pile-up on the M6 Motorway near Junction 12 at some point in the early 1980s. I told Fletcher that I was not at all impressed, and that he should get on with the story at hand, as I had plenty of other things that I could be doing on a Saturday afternoon, instead of listening to him waffle on endlessly about dead car-crash victims on the M6. And so, I sat back and listened intently as Fletcher told his weird tales, while messily and simultaneously devouring a greasy plate of sausages, eggs, bacon and fried bread, all topped off with about half a bottle of *Daddies Sauce* and a mountain of salt.

Aside from being mad and warped, Fletcher was infinitely dangerous, too. But first a bit of background: it must be remembered that this all took place back in was 1989. There was certainly no Internet to speak of as such; the multitude of magazines on the paranormal that would flood the news-stands of *WH Smith* and *Menzies* in the mid-to-late 1990s, such as *Alien Encounters, Uri Geller's Encounters, UFO Magazine, Sightings, Enigma, UFO Reality*, and *X-Factor*, were not even a glint in *anyone's* eye; and books on subjects such as aliens, Bigfoot, and the Loch Ness Monster sold to what was without doubt an infinitely small, fringe element of the British book-reading population. As a result, while it is true to say that there were most certainly a fair number of people around the country doing a lot of good, solid research into the myriad mysteries of this world and beyond, there was no real, unified scene of the type that would surface in the 1990s and at the height of Mulder and Scully mania.

Whereas in today's world of instant information, any and all data of a Fortean nature can be in the hands of the entire community within a matter of a few minutes if not a few seconds even, such was most definitely not the case back in 1989. Certainly, there were those newsletters, self-published fanzines, and the occasional semi-professional publications such as the early incarnation of *Fortean Times*, the *Bufora Journal* and *Flying Saucer Review*. But more often than not, what was going on, for example, in the West Country of a 'big cat' nature might remain largely unknown to those investigating a UFO encounter in Scotland, and vice-versa, for weeks at a time.

So, what is my point, you may ask? Well, it's this: due to the relatively fractured, and somewhat isolated, nature of the nation's Fortean scene back then, Fletcher had skillfully (I have to give him that much, at least) wormed his way into the living-rooms and personal lives of several key figures within that same scene, and he had begun to systematically blackmail them; and all without other members of said community having any real inkling of what on earth he was up to. Indeed, it was the very fact that each of these individuals had little or no contact with each other in what was then an utterly email-free era that meant Fletcher's actions went largely undetected.

I found it highly puzzling that Fletcher practically bragged to me – someone he didn't even know from Adam - about his supposed activities, and how he had 'found out secrets about certain people that some would kill for'. He *never* named names, but earnestly maintained to me that British Forteana was rife with Irish Republican Army (IRA) supporters, 'professional football hooligans', 'dangerous perverts and sexual freaks', as well as a certain person who had been firmly busted for siphoning off thousands of pounds from his employer, before changing his name in the late 1970s, and then emerging into the Fortean scene in 1981 as a leading player.

From the brief yet admittedly intriguing details that Fletcher confided in me, I gained the distinct impression that such controversial data was seemingly coming to him from someone in the local Police Force – and maybe, perhaps, even the same person who had allegedly supplied him with that disturbing imagery of car-crash victims some years earlier – if his controversial story could even be believed at all, of course.

But Fletcher was certainly no ordinary blackmailer: indeed, he had no interest in money, whatsoever. That much was readily apparent to me from his appearance and overwhelming stench. Rather, he had 'threatened' several leading figures in Forteana 'with exposure' unless they provided him with that one thing that he so dearly desired most of all: information.

As a result, Fletcher's home on Rugeley's Pear Tree Estate, which I would finally get to visit some ten days later, was filled to the brim with photocopies of literally thousands of pages of case-files, interviews, reports, books, and more; the majority of which (so Fletcher told me, at least) was supplied to him by the unfortunate souls that he had got his deep claws into – and to their considerable cost, too. He told me with much evil glee how he could, at the very merest of whims, telephone certain characters in the field of the unexplained and demand this or request that; and that if they knew what was good for them, then they would seek to obtain it for him at the very earliest of opportunities.

It must be said that I always seriously doubted the long and convoluted tale that Fletcher was telling me. Rather, for most of the time I considered it little more than a weak and pathetic attempt to boost his own fragile ego and his undoubted disturbed mind, and thereby create for himself a degree of self-esteem, mystery, and mythology. But, nevertheless duly intrigued, I elected to firmly put Fletcher to the test and I asked him to see what he could find out for me on the Man-Monkey of the Shropshire Union Canal and its exploits of January 1879. He told me that he was wholly unacquainted with the story – which was not really surprising to me at all, given its relatively obscure nature back then. But, after I mailed him the relevant photo-copied pages from the Bord's *Alien Animals*, he good-naturedly agreed to see what he could do for me. It has to be said that I hardly held my breath in much anticipation at all; but I was most well and truly floored when, about six weeks later - and after I had practically forgotten all about him - Fletcher mailed me a large envelope of material.

I was due to go on holiday with a bunch of mates in a few days time, and it was to be approximately another six weeks before I was even able to get back to Fletcher. I was shocked, to say the very least, when after getting no reply at all by telephone for a while, I finally drove over again to Rugeley's Pear Tree Estate, only to be told by his nosy next-door neighbour who was lurking around that Fletcher had died suddenly three weeks earlier. That utterly mad soul was gone. And, unfortunately, the admittedly intriguing secrets of his life as an alleged Fortean blackmailer were gone, too. I did learn from the woman who lived on the other side of Fletcher, however, that someone from a paranormal research group somewhere in the vicinity of the Potteries had turned up right after Fletcher's death, had claimed all of his files and his books, had summarily loaded them into the back of an old Transit van, and had then quickly roared out of town, never to be seen again.

But I did, at least, have that intriguing batch of material that Fletcher had mailed to me. And, thus, my investigation of the Man-Monkey of Bridge 39 could now well and truly begin in earnest.

CHAPTER IV
THE SHUGBOROUGH AFFAIR

Situated near to the picturesque little Cannock Chase hamlet of Milford, Shugborough Hall is both a large and renowned country house that serves as the ancestral home of the Earls of Lichfield; and its spacious grounds are connected to the nearby village of Great Haywood by the Essex Bridge, which was built during the Middle Ages. Around 1750, the hall was enlarged, and then yet again at the beginning of the 1800s. Today, Shugborough Hall is open to the general public and boasts a working farm museum that dates back to 1805, and which is complete with a watermill, kitchens and a dairy.

Interestingly, the grounds of Shugborough Hall are also home to something known as the Shepherd's Monument, upon which can be found a very strange inscription, and one which many students of the puzzle believe contains a secret code that identifies the alleged resting place of none other than the Holy Grail. The Shepherd's Monument is not the only such construction of note on the grounds of the sprawling hall: The Tower of Winds; the Cat's Monument; and the Doric Temple also have pride of place.

And if the data provided by the mysterious (and now dead) Fletcher could be conclusively confirmed, Shugborough Hall was also inextricably tied to the saga of the Man-Beast of Bridge 39.

The package of material sent to me by Fletcher contained photocopies of the relevant pages from the Bord's *Alien Animals* book, as well as those from Charlotte S. Burne's *Shropshire Folklore* title of 1883. But it also contained something else, too: namely no less than eight pages of hand-written notes that carefully summarised an interview (undertaken in 1987 by a man then living in the Potteries, and who was attached to a north Staffordshire paranormal group that existed at the time) with a former grounds-man at Shugborough Hall who had heard some decidedly Man-Monkey-like tales from within the boundaries of the very hall itself.

It transpired that the grounds-man – whose name was unfortunately blacked-out on the photo-copied versions of the relevant files - had been employed at Shugborough Hall from the late 1970s to the early 1980s and had confided in the Potteries-based group that, at some point in the early part of 1981, distinctly strange events had taken place late at night at the old hall. On no less than five occasions – and specifically between February and April of that year – an undisclosed number of the many geese and ducks that frequented the pleasant waters of Shugborough Hall were found decapitated, and with their bodies laid out in 'what looked like a witchcraft ceremony'.

Precisely how the interviewee had been able to determine with both confidence and accuracy what a 'witchcraft ceremony' might or might not actually look like was not made clear to the group, however; and, as far as I was able to tell at least, they seemingly – and somewhat bafflingly - did not even think to ask such an important question of the man anyway.

There was far more to come, however: on at least two occasions strange, loud, guttural noises had been heard coming from one particular tree-shrouded area of the grounds; and a large, hairy man-like 'thing' had been observed by a shocked employee bounding at high speed across the lawns long after the sun had gone down - and specifically heading in the direction of the winding waters that continue to run through the Shugborough Hall estate to this day. Indeed, the same employee had recalled hearing a loud splashing noise in the immediate aftermath of the sighting, which suggested strongly to one and all that the creature had actually launched itself into those same waters.

According to the documentation provided to me by Fletcher, the Potteries-based group had travelled to Shugborough Hall on two occasions in 1987 (once in late June and then again in mid-July) to secure both photographs and interviews. And while obtaining pictures of the locations where the sightings, killings and (potential) rituals and rites were carried out presented no problems at all of course, undertaking corroborating interviews to actually try and confirm the details of the story proved to be somewhat less than satisfactory. For example, two additional members of the staff who seemingly knew at least *something* about the mysterious affair had moved on to other jobs by the time that a meaningful study of the case could be launched, and specifically declined to be interviewed; something which duly left the group with just the one, original source of the story.

Fletcher's files revealed to me that the grounds-man had been interviewed deeply by the group; and during the course of the interviews he had alluded to semi-veiled warnings made to him by senior staff at Shugborough Hall not to talk about the killings and beheadings, the rites and rituals, and most certainly not the sightings of the wild, hairy man-beast – in the event that it would likely be considered bad for the tourist business (frankly, I personally thought that it would have all been great fun for the tourists; but hey - that's just my opinion). Nevertheless, the man *did* at least confirm that a decision had been taken at the very highest level 'not to report anything to the police', and further asserted that 'everything' was dealt with strictly in-house; aside from a visit by an individual ('some vet') whose services were occasionally used to treat the smaller animals that lived at the hall, and who reportedly made a detailed examination of the dead water-fowl.

The files also revealed several other things: namely, that the man-beast seen running wildly in the grounds exuded a foul smell that was somewhat akin to 'rotting veg'; that not a single one of the dead birds appeared to have put up a fight before decapitation (for example, there were no large piles of feathers laying around, no blood, and the birds looked to have been 'cleanly cut' and not torn open); and that the man had heard, from a colleague and friend, of 'something like this happening here before, in the 1960s, with a monkey running around'.

Well, barely one week after digesting all of this admittedly intriguing data, I decided it was well and truly high time to pay a visit to Shugborough Hall for myself. And so it was that while getting a cup of tea and a cake in the hall's café, I somewhat less than tactfully brought up with the staff the details of the weird events of early 1981 as described in the files provided to me by Fletcher.

I have to say that I was hardly surprised by the reception that my controversial and odd questions received: namely one that was a mixture of puzzlement and amusement – as well as a small amount of concern that a nutter was wildly roaming their historic hall. It was a typical and unfortunate reception of the type that I had been on the receiving end of many times before; and one that I would be on the receiving end of many times again. Such are the trials and tribulations of a Fortean investigator, unfortunately. Nevertheless, the staff had to admit that they *did* find the whole thing *very* intriguing, and eventually they regaled me with entertaining tales of other spectral entities said to haunt Shugborough Hall – although, it must be said that these were all of the classic 'Grey Lady' type phenomenon, and most certainly not of a hairy and Bigfoot-like nature.

And while I could never really prove a direct connection, one of the employees *did* recall a weird event that had supposedly occurred around four months previous to my visit in which a horse had apparently been violently 'slashed' on its back legs in a fashion that looked suspiciously like the work of a wild animal, such as a 'big cat'. Unfortunately, there were no more salient details available; and so, therefore, I could do very little more than merely log the story, in the event that further corroborating data might ultimately one day surface. Unfortunately, it never did.

It must be said that this aspect of my Man-Monkey investigation was particularly frustrating and perplexing, and in equal measures, too: I did finally manage to track down the current whereabouts of the several investigators from the Potteries who had travelled to Shugborough Hall back in 1987 – but who all steadfastly refused to share any more of their findings, citing the fact that they were *their* files, and *no-one else* was *ever* allowed access to them. Sadly, this somewhat ridiculous and pompous attitude is all-too-prevalent within many – if indeed not *all* – aspects of Forteana. For some very odd and truly unfathomable reason, so many researchers just love to generate filing-cabinets full of data; yet those same researchers are so often curiously unwilling to share that same data with like-minded souls, who might actually be able to contribute something worthwhile. So it goes.

Although, I have to say with some amusement that I ended up being on the receiving end of several late-night, frantic telephone-calls from a certain long-time member of the group, highly worried about the fact that I had been liaising with Fletcher and that he had shared with me at least some of their 'secret files'. While it was never made expressly clear to me, I strongly suspected that the caller in question was probably the chief source of the files supplied to me by my now-dead informant, and he was expressing deep concern about what I was going to do with them. Well, if he's still around and reading these words, now he knows.

And with that distinct lack of cooperation in evidence throughout this aspect of my investigation, as well as the complete and utter dead-ends that I was faced with at Shugborough Hall, and the absence of even a name for the main source of this particular story, I was reluctantly forced to relegate this aspect of my quest to one of those avenues that - as interesting and eye-opening as it most certainly was - seemed to offer far more intriguing and uncertain questions than it ever really did satisfactory answers.

It is worth noting, however, that there are other, verifiable examples of domesticated animals being killed in the area and under very weird circumstances. For example, on June 6, 1931, the *Cannock Advertiser* newspaper reported the following, from the nearby locale of Hatherton: 'A ewe and a lamb were killed last week when a bolt of lightning hit the large ash tree that they were standing next to. The animals that belonged to farmer Mr. Gripton of Hatherton fell victim to the storm, which also included heavy rain, and hail-stones. The large ash tree was struck at the trunk, where the bark was stripped. *The farmer described how it looked like a ball of fire came from the clouds in a zigzag manner* [Note from the author: Italics mine]. Many other trees were reported hit by lightning during the storm.'

Undoubtedly, this was a classic example of that rare phenomenon known as ball-lightning; yet the fact that it should have struck – and killed at least two animals – in an area already steeped in distinct high-strangeness, is both unusual and noteworthy indeed.

CHAPTER V
WALKING THE WOODS

Approximately two weeks or so after digging into the mysteri-ous affair of Shugborough Hall, I finally headed out to the location where all of the monumental fuss had allegedly taken place more than a century before. I have always been a firm believer that the only way to really conduct an investigation, of *any-thing*, is to actually get out there – into the field, so to speak – and do it properly, in-person. Merely downloading reams of electronic data from the safe and sterile confines of the Internet, and then having the unmitigated gall to pass it off as 'research', doth not an investigation define – at least, not in my book it doesn't. And I most certainly, and sincerely, hope that it doesn't in yours, either.

And so thus it was that on a bright and sunny Sunday morning, I set off for that cursed stretch of canal, and my quarry (if I was *really* lucky, I mused to myself): the Man-Monkey. Negotiating the wind-ing and narrow, tree-enveloped roads of the area, and finding the precise site of the encounter of 1879 presented no problems to me at all: the Bords had included a black-and-white photograph of the rele-vant stretch of old road-bridge in their *Alien Animals* book. And, in one of those decidedly synchronistic moments that seem to utterly bedevil those of us with distinctly Fortean pursuits, I was quickly able to deduce upon arriving at the bridge in question that I had ac-tually driven along the *exact* stretch of road on more than several oc-casions when working as a van-driver in the late 1980s, and while making paint and wallpaper deliveries in that very area.

Although most Internet-based sites today refer to the unidentified hairy entity as the 'Man-Monkey of Ranton', in reality, as I was able to determine upon arriving at the site, the encounter of January 1879 cited by Charlotte S. Burne within the pages of her *Shropshire Folk-lore* book had actually occurred much closer to the village of Wood-seaves. But that was not all. I had often wondered to myself how something so devilish and downright extraordinary as the Man-

Monkey – if the dark story had any truth to it, of course – could so easily and successfully hide itself in the vicinity of a stretch of canal that was, presumably, wide open to the general public.

Well, on arriving at the scene, that question was very quickly and very graphically answered for me. As I approached the relevant bridge – having recognised it from the photograph contained in the Bord's *Alien Animals* book – I slowed down my old *Ford Capri*, and proceeded to pull into a small, dusty parking-space on the far left side of the bridge. I exited the vehicle, with both camera and tape-recorder in-hand to record for posterity both my thoughts and crucial imagery. Indeed, I am very glad that I did so, since I am now able to firmly draw upon that material evidence for the benefit of you, the reader.

The image that the story of the Man-Monkey creates is one of a wide-open canal, easily accessible and viewable to one and all. But, that is actually far from the truth. The road-bridge that was the scene of all the monumental fuss way back in 1879 is, in reality, situated a considerable height above the canal. As a result, therefore, a person has to negotiate a small gate at the edge of the heavily wooded road, and then head down a steep, dusty, and well-worn pathway to the canal waters deep below. Not only that: the entire stretch of canal at issue is surrounded by thick woods that envelop the dark waters of the Shropshire Union Canal with a dense canopy of foliage that even in broad daylight creates a scene and atmosphere of distinct high-strangeness. Indeed, arriving at the edge of the canal generates an odd feeling of isolation, too – and one that is not at all unlike the famous 'Oz-Factor' coined by British ufologist Jenny Randles – and a deep impression of leaving the modern world far, far behind. And, certainly, this is made all the more distinctive by virtue of the fact that the location is situated well within an area of countryside that has remained practically unchanged for centuries, and far away from the hustle and bustle of traffic, towns, and such like.

I walked the heavily wooded canal for something like an hour in each direction, carefully scanning the dense trees, taking countless photographs, staring deep into those hypnotically-enchanting waters, and finally coming to the startling conclusion that the tale of the Man-Monkey might not just be a fable, after all. Indeed, it might be all too real; disturbingly so, in fact. And with that intriguing thought firmly locked in my mind, I duly headed back to my car, and a journey home via the dark woods of the Cannock Chase.

It was not long after the death of Fletcher that my fraught relationship with the world of 9-to-5 came to a crashing and decisive end. By now completely and utterly tired of working for the slave state of the monstrous Thatcher regime, I defiantly vowed that hell would freeze over before I ever returned; and I decided that from that moment on I was going to do exactly what I wanted to do, on my own terms, and most certainly not on anyone else's. Having had an overwhelmingly riotous time while working on *Zero* a few years earlier, I decided that I would try and combine my passion for the unknown and the paranormal with the enthusiasm for writing that I had cultivated on the aforementioned *Zero*. As a direct result, I thus embarked upon the first, tentative steps of a career as a freelance writer and author – one that continues to this very day, I am pleased to say.

And, although it was most certainly somewhat of a struggle at first to adequately make ends meet (on far more than one occasion, as I can still graphically recall, my hand would slip down the side of the settee in search of pennies), it was the sheer drive and dogged determination to stay away from the 9-to-5 world that kept me going; and I was eventually able to live fairly comfortably on the income that I was slowly starting to generate from freelance writing; the vast majority of which, at that time at least, had absolutely nothing whatsoever to do with Forteana at all.

I have to confess at this point that over the next couple of years my studies into the legend of the Man-Monkey took somewhat of a backseat – once again, and to my regret, I now freely admit. Around 1991 I had taken the decision to embark upon the writing of a book on my researches into the long and complicated history of the British Ministry of Defence's involvement in the UFO puzzle; and which ultimately culminated in the September 1997 publication of my book *A Covert Agenda: The British Government's UFO Top Secrets Exposed*. Nevertheless, from time to time intriguing reports would still continue to reach me of dark encounters with hairy man-beasts in both Shropshire and Staffordshire; and whenever such reports did surface I would never be too far behind. One such classic report came from Jackie Houghton.

Back in 1995, Jackie was a waitress then living in a Cannock bed-sit and working at a restaurant in the nearby town of Stafford. At around 1.00 a.m. on February 18 of that year, she had been driving across the Cannock Chase, and along the main road that links the towns of Rugeley and Cannock, after her shift at the restaurant was finally over. As she approached the turning for the village of Slitting Mill, however, Jackie was suddenly forced to quickly and violently swerve the car and only narrowly avoided collision with a large, shambling creature that had chosen to step out into the road at a distance of about two hundred yards from her. Considering that she was travelling at a high speed, said Jackie, it was nothing less than a marvel that she didn't hit the hairy thing. The encounter had lasted just a few scant seconds, but she *had* caught sight of the animal in the headlights of her vehicle, and was absolutely one-hundred-per-cent certain that it was both man-like and tall, very hairy, and weirdest of all: possessed a pair of self-illuminating, glowing red eyes. In an instant, said Jackie, the huge beast had vanished into the darkness, leaving her distinctly shaken and highly stirred. And then there was the man named Gavin.

Gavin, who I was able to meet personally, claimed a truly sensational encounter with a Bigfoot-like entity at one of the Cannock Chase's most famous attractions: namely, the Glacial Boulder. Made out of granite, the boulder is both large and impressive. It is also made highly curious by virtue of the illuminating fact that there are *no* natural granite out-crops anywhere in the area – at all. Indeed, the nearest rock of this specific type can be found within the picturesque confines of the Lake District, which is more than 120 miles to the north, and on Dartmoor, Devonshire, no less than 165 miles to the south-west. The boulder itself, however, has been matched conclusively to a rocky outcrop at Cniffel in Dumfries & Galloway, which is over 170 miles from the Chase in the Southern Uplands of Scotland. At some point during the last Ice Age, it is now generally accepted, the boulder was apparently carried by the great glaciers down the length of the British Isles and to its present location – and what would prove to be its final resting place - on the Cannock Chase.

As Gavin breathlessly explained his sensational story to me, it was on a winter's night in 1997, when he and his girlfriend were parked in his car near the boulder, doing what courting couples have always done since the invention of the automobile, when his girlfriend suddenly let out a loud and hysterical scream: standing atop the boulder was a large hairy man, waving his arms in a wild, crazed fashion at the star-lit sky. Gavin quickly jumped into the front seat of the car and floored the accelerator. Tires spun, dirt flew into the air, and the car shot away at high speed; but not before the creature supposedly succeeded in jumping onto the bonnet of his car. For five minutes, it valiantly hung on, before finally being thrown to the ground. Gavin looked in his rear-view mirror and was horrified to see that the creature was already back on its feet and running at high-speed into the depths of the surrounding countryside.

In fairness to the more sceptical minded, it must be said at this point that several other people who have also met Gavin are convinced that his tale is simply that: merely a tale (of the very tallest variety) and nothing more. For his part, Gavin has been careful – time and again - to point out in response that he has nothing to gain – and absolutely everything to lose – by fabricating such a strange and unbelievable story. And in that respect he is most certainly not wrong: claiming to all and sundry that you have seen a Bigfoot-type entity roaming around the Cannock Chase at night is, unfortunately, unlikely to result in anything other than the rolling of eyes, a distinct shaking of the head, and overwhelming hoots of both derision and laughter. There was something else that I could not ignore or fail to recognise, either: Gavin's story contained the key ingredient of the account of the unfortunate witness at Woodseaves in 1879: namely, that of a wild, violent, hair-covered man-beast that seemed to have a particular penchant for launching itself at carts, cars, horses and their unsuspecting drivers, riders and passengers. And Gavin's story, that seemed to closely parallel the incident of 1879 at Woodseaves, would most certainly not be the last of this type to catch my keen attention.

Peggy Baker's tale was equally as intriguing – and perhaps more so given its location. In the winter of 1997, Peggy had been driving through the village of Ranton with her daughter, Kathleen, when at around 11.30 p.m., the pair – just like so many others – was shocked and scared witless by the surreal sight of a shambling, hairy man-beast that loomed out of the darkened fringes of the roadside, 'threw its arms around in the air', and proceeded to 'shout at us, like a big roar'. Not surprisingly, the terrified mother and daughter did not once slow down to get a closer look at the creature; but instead fled the scene with the utmost haste.

And with the Baker's account now firmly fixed in our minds, perhaps it is time for a word or several about the historic village of Ranton: not only is it situated within almost literal spitting distance of Bridge 39 where all of the action occurred on that winter's night in 1879, but it is a locale that is literally chocked to the brim with a wide and varied range of weird and seemingly paranormal activity.

The History, Gazetteer and Directory of Staffordshire of 1851 described Ranton thus: 'Ranton, or Ronton, is a small scattered village, five miles W of Stafford, comprising within its parish the scattered hamlets of Extolls, Long Compton, Park Nook, and including 320 inhabitants, and about 2670 acres of land, belonging chiefly to the Earl of Lichfield, and Francis Eld, Esq., and the former is lord of the manor, which, at the time of the Norman Conquest, was held by Goderick, a Saxon nobleman, and afterwards by the Noels and Harcourts. Swynfen Jones, Esq., and a few smaller owners have estates in the parish. About a mile W of the village is Ranton Abbey, an extra parochial liberty of 700 acres belonging to the Earl of Lichfield. The ancient abbey was founded by Robert Fitz-Noel, in the reign of Henry II, for regular canons of the order of St. Augustine. Considerable remains of the abbey are still standing, including a lofty well-built tower, and the outer walls of the church. The abbey liberty contains 28 inhabitants and the Abbey House which is the seat of ED Moore, Esq.'

Today, Ranton has changed very little, as can be firmly evidenced by the fact that according to the national census of 1991, the village's population had by then only risen to four-hundred-and-fifteen. Yet, the amount of high-strangeness in the area has certainly been considerable – and that's putting it mildly indeed. Back in the 1920s, for example, there had occurred in Ranton a close encounter of the pixie kind, according to an elderly (and now, unfortunately, deceased) lady who personally related her account to me in 2000. It was in 1929, the woman recalled, and she was then five years of age when she witnessed the startling sight of a group of tiny pixies, all adorned in dark green clothing, and all prancing wildly around the large and mighty oak tree that stood at the foot of her parents' back-garden.

But what had begun as an overwhelmingly friendly encounter, with smiling little creatures that playfully tipped their hats in the direction of the entranced young girl, became far more sinister when the atmosphere changed dramatically and the little folk mutated into malevolent, sinister figures that, the old woman explained, slowly began to move towards her in a 'stalking' fashion, complete with menacing frowns on their suddenly-wizened faces. Needless to say, the petrified witness fled for the safety of her home; never again to see the strange, unearthly parade.

Then there was the close encounter with a glowing-eyed 'black panther' in the early 1990s, that a resident of Ranton had seen bounding across the road in front of her late one Friday night. But surely Ranton's most famous story of a distinctly paranormal nature was that of Jessie Roestenberg, who in October 1954 claimed to have witnessed with her children a classic George Adamski-type flying saucer-style object over Ranton that had built into its side a large 'observation window', through which could be viewed a number of human-like entities with long-blonde hair. In other words, the whole area surrounding Bridge 39 seemed to be a veritable hot-bed of over-the-top weirdness. And the reports of local sightings of hairy man-beasts just kept on coming in the 1990s.

Submitted to the website of the United States-based group *The Gulf Coast Bigfoot Research Organisation* by researcher Bobby Hamilton was the following account from a confidential source, who had reported seeing a strange, man-like creature on the Cannock Chase in September 1998. With three friends, the source was journeying by car along the A34 road between Stafford and Cannock. It was about 12.30 a.m., and in the area of the Cannock woods, when all four simultaneously noticed something distinctly strange just off the side of the road.

In the words of the chief source of the account: 'It was a star-filled night, clear, but dark and we were all in the car driving home, happily chatting and joking. Suddenly we all fell dead serious, the people in the back sat forward and we all pointed to the same shape. It was a tall man-like figure, sort of crouching forward. As we passed, it turned and looked straight at us. In my own words I would describe it as around 6 feet 8 inches tall, legs thicker than two of mine, very strong looking and with a darkish, blacky-brown coat. I just could not explain it and I still get goose-bumps thinking of it.'

The informant advised Hamilton that: 'No one would be out there on the night playing about; it was very cold that night...I can identify deer in thick bush; this was open. I hope this is of some help; it is the absolute truth to the best of my memory. Why make up something like that?'

To which I can only add these two words: why, indeed?

I suppose that by this time I knew deep in my heart and mind that writing a pamphlet - or even, perhaps, a book - on the saga of the Man-Monkey (as well as the many and varied, additional encounters with beast-men in both Shropshire and Staffordshire) was at least *somewhat* feasible; and I thought back to my experiences out at the Shropshire Union Canal, the notable witness testimony I had secured, as well as the weird revelations that had surfaced from the mysteriously departed Fletcher. But much more data was going to be required before I could even begin to contemplate working on the book that you now find yourself reading.

CHAPTER VI
THE CULT OF THE MOON-BEAST

One person who I really have to thank for putting me hot on the trail of the Man-Monkey is Mike Lockley, the editor of the *Chase Post* newspaper – which covers the Staffordshire town of Cannock and the aforementioned Cannock Chase forest. I had first met Mike in 1999 when I was busily promoting my third UFO book, *Cosmic Crashes: The Incredible Story of the UFOs That Fell to Earth*. As the book included no less than two weird tales of alleged UFO crashes deep in the heart of the Cannock Chase, I quickly contacted Mike in an attempt to give the newly-published book some local – and hopefully welcome - publicity. Needless to say, he was more than keen to do so; and, therefore, over coffee in the summer of that same year we met and planned a series of articles for the newspaper – chiefly about the book and the local UFO scene, the latter with the help of Irene Bott, then-President of the Staffordshire UFO Group.

I kept in touch with Mike on a regular basis, keen as I was to carefully continue to cultivate contacts within both the local and national media. And it was in early 2000 that Mike asked me if I would be interested in co-writing with Irene a regular column for the *Chase Post* that would focus specifically upon the paranormal mysteries of the Cannock Chase. I replied that, yes indeed, I most certainly would be interested.

And so it was that for the better part of a year Irene and I plundered our considerable files, various archives, and local libraries in search of strange and dark tales with which to hopefully entertain the good folk of Cannock for our column – that had the slightly naff title of *The C-Files* and that saw me playing the role of Mulder to Irene's Scully. Remember, of course: this was 2000, and *The X-Files* mania that had helped me pay my bills and buy my daily quota of *Carls-*

berg Special Brew throughout the entirety of this halcyon, barmy, and sadly now-gone, period hadn't quite run out of steam yet.

Most of our articles were focused upon those mysterious events and encounters that had occurred directly on the Cannock Chase – namely sightings of UFOs and aliens, big cats of the puma variety, ghosts and spectres, and even the occasional paranormal black dog or two. But, after a few short months, we found that it was becoming increasingly difficult to keep coming up with brand new stories - on a weekly basis, no less - that exclusively dealt just with the town of Cannock itself and the surrounding Cannock Chase woods. And with this thorny and tricky issue firmly fixed in my mind, I decided that we simply had to broaden the scope of the articles a bit; and so Irene and I duly spread our Fortean wings. Thus it was that in the summer of 2000 an article appeared from us in the *Chase Post* that detailed the remarkable events of that long-gone night of 1879 when the Man-Monkey first burst forth out of those dark, shadowy woods at Bridge 39 on the Shropshire Union Canal.

Titled *Man-Monkey and Big Cats* and published in the *Chase Post* on August 31, 2000, the one-page article outlined the essential facts pertaining to the ominous tale – as well as revealing the notable details of a new big-cat encounter in the region. As always, I ensured that my telephone number accompanied the article, in the event that anyone wanted to get in touch and relate to me their own tale. And get in touch, they most assuredly did.

When the article appeared, all hell broke loose – metaphorically speaking, at least. I was quite literally inundated with telephone calls from a whole variety of local newspapers and radio-stations, all wanting to know more about the hairy man-beast of the Shropshire Union Canal. Needless to say, I was happy to oblige and spoke in endless detail about the case on Radio Stoke, Radio WM and on countless other stations. As a result – and as I had earnestly hoped would be the case – word began to get out in the Midlands, and elsewhere as it transpired, that I was looking deeply into the events of January 1879, and a considerable number of people with alleged personal and first-hand knowledge of the Man-Monkey and its daring and diabolical exploits phoned me up to relate the details of what turned out be truly remarkable accounts.

Certainly, the most memorable story of that initial batch was that of Rob Lea. Rob had phoned me on the same day that the article had appeared in the *Post* and advised me, in somewhat excited, yet also deeply concerned, tones that he had been diligently chasing *another* story for a lengthy period of time that, he had come to learn, was indirectly – or maybe even directly - tied-in with that of the Man-Monkey. Well, that alone was most certainly enough for me to arrange a face-to-face meeting with him – which would take place two days later at a pub in the nearby village of Milford.

Rob had seen my photograph in the *Chase Post* and proceeded to wave amiably from his seat as I stood at the bar and ordered a pint. I nodded, got him a refill of what I could clearly see was a half-full pint of Guinness, and headed over to the table. Rob was a Goth, decked out in black jeans, chunky boots, and a long black-leather coat, through which peeked a battered *Siouxsie and the Banshees* t-shirt. A badge displaying Charles Manson's face was pinned to Rob's coat-collar; and a small amount of redness surrounded a nose-ring that I determined was newly acquired.

The *very* painfully-thin and pasty-faced Rob viewed himself as quite the Sherlock Holmes; and after listening to his tale, I had to agree. Either that or he was an insane fantasist or con-merchant of truly infinite proportions. Frankly, even to this very day I'm still not sure which scenario is the correct one. But his long and winding tale was most certainly not one that could be ignored, to say the least.

Rob told me that as a direct result of a macabre incident that had occurred in the early spring of 1989 on a Newport-based farm that was owned by his family, he had developed a deep and personal interest in stories of animal mutilation. Refreshingly, I learned, he was not some rabid *X-Files*-style devotee looking to validate tales that extraterrestrial Grey's were busily stealing bovine body-parts and secretly transferring them to some *James Bond*-like underground base in New Mexico for who-knew-what bizarre purposes. Or worse still: that they were taking mutilated hedgehogs to a secure underground installation, deep below Porton Down, Wiltshire. No: Rob's investigations had taken a far more eye-opening and significant path.

It was in the latter part of August 1989, recalled Rob as he took a careful sip from his pint of Guinness, when his father had arisen early one morning to find five of his sheep slaughtered under highly unusual and shocking circumstances: laid out in a circle, all five had had their throats cut, with several of their major organs piled high in the middle of the circle. Thoughts of devil-worship inevitably flooded through his father's frantic mind, said Rob. Unsurprisingly, the family quickly telephoned the local police, who promptly came out with surprising speed and filed a report, and quietly urged the family not to give the incident too much publicity under *any* circumstances. No answers were ever forthcoming, however, and the eerie event was never repeated. But it had left a deep and dark impression on the then-teenaged Rob. Of course, this was merely a tale; and it must be said that Rob was highly concerned about revealing to me the precise location of the farm in question. However, he surprised me with a true ace that he had been hiding up his sleeve all of this time.

Rob smiled, reached below the table, and produced a black briefcase which he duly placed on to the table-top. As he flipped its brass-coloured locks, I moved the glasses and the ashtray aside to allow for more room, and I sat back, waiting to see what would develop. From within the confines of a large, padded envelope, Rob pulled out seven, 6 x 4, 35mm, colour-photographs that graphically displayed the scene of utter carnage at his family's farm more than a decade earlier. In other words, and if nothing else, that part of the story could at least be firmly validated. But that was only the very beginning of things – as I had strongly suspected it might be as soon as Rob had begun to spin his unusual tale to me.

Rob continued and admitted to me that when he first began digging into the animal mutilation mystery he *was*, for a mercifully short while at least, an adherent of the theory that dastardly extraterrestrials just *might* be at work. I groaned ever so slightly – but, then again, I *had* seriously considered such a possibility myself in the paranoia-driven Mulder 'n' Scully era; so I most certainly had no room to talk at all. As time progressed, however, Rob found that, in many ways, something far more disturbing than alien visitations was afoot.

By the late 1990s, said Rob - and specifically during the time period in which *UFO Magazine's* Tony Dodd and UFO researcher David Cayton were making highly controversial waves in the field of animal mutilation research in jolly old England - he had quietly and carefully travelled the length and breadth of the British Isles in hot pursuit of the answers to the puzzle, and had inadvertently stumbled upon a sinister group of people based near Bristol – that Rob had grandly dubbed 'The Cult of the Moon-Beast' – that, he asserted to me, were using slaughtered farm animals and even house-hold pets in ancient rites and archaic rituals. The purpose of those rites and rituals, said Rob continuing, was to use the sacrificed unfortunates as a means of conjuring up werewolf-style entities from some vile neth-erworld, and that would then be dispatched to commit God-knows-what atrocities on behalf of their masters in the Cult of the Moon-Beast.

Well, this was certainly a good story. No: it was a damned, *great* story. But was it even remotely true? And, even if it was, what the hell did it have to do with the Man-Monkey? Again, Rob impressed me when he pulled yet another surprise out of his trusty brief-case: namely, an audio-tape-recording of an interview with an elderly resi-dent of Newport named Sam who had told Rob in 1995 that, as a child in the 1930s, he – Sam – had heard unearthly tales in town of a spate of supposed werewolf sightings that had occurred in the 1910s at none other than the *exact* same bridge on the Shropshire Union Canal where the Man-Monkey had been seen in 1879 – something that will take on even greater significance in the chapter that follows.

Well, it transpired that Rob had been stealthily watching the activi-ties of the Cult of the Moon-Beast – which, he stressed several times, was merely a term that he, himself, had applied to this closely-knit group of individuals that numbered around fifteen – for nigh-on seven years by the time we met. He actually had no firm idea of the group's real name at all; or even if it *had* a name. Although the cult was firmly based in Bristol, said Rob, its members were spread both far and wide, with at least four hailing from Ipswich; two from none other than Cannock; two from the city of Exeter; one from Tavistock, Devonshire; and five from Bromley, Kent. And one, he knew, had a Scottish accent.

Rob related to me how he had clandestinely and doggedly tracked the movements of the group and had personally – albeit stealthily – viewed no less than three of their dark practices: one of which, he said, had occurred in early 2000 near the Ingrestre Park Golf Club on the Cannock Chase.

'And what exactly is this group doing with these werewolves that it summons up? And where is it summoning them up from?' I asked Rob.

He had a reply ready and waiting for me. According to Rob, the Man-Monkey of 1879 had the same point of origin as the werewolves that in 2000 were being darkly manipulated by the Cult of the Moon-Beast. Rob said that they both came from a realm or dimension that co-existed with ours and that at times 'combined' with ours at random and in a fashion that defied prediction. However, he added that certain locales around the country allowed for a doorway or portal to be opened to order, if one followed the correct, ancient rites, rituals and 'rules of animal sacrifice', of which the Cult of the Moon-Beast apparently had a deep awareness. Numerous such portals existed in Devon, Cornwall, and Staffordshire, Rob assured me in an earnest fashion.

'Yes, but again why are they doing this? What's the purpose?' I wanted to know.

Rob looked me square in the face: 'Murder.'

'Murder,' I replied, in a tone that was a statement rather than a question.

Rob nodded eagerly and related to me that the werewolves in question were not physical, flesh-and-blood-style beings in the way that we, at least, understand things. Rather, they were a form of non-physical intelligence that could take on the appearance of whatever was in the mind's eye of the beholder. Their real form, said Rob, was that of small, balls of light that would haunt the byways and woods of old England. But, via interaction with the human mind, they could present themselves in the form of several, specific archetypes: a hairy man (be it ape-man or wolf-man); a giant bird-like creature; a large dog; a giant cat; or a slithering, eel-like entity.

Of course, these were without any doubt at all the staple creatures of fortean zoology: Bigfoot, the Owlman, the Black Dogs of British folklore, the alien big cats that so many people were seeing throughout Britain, and the ridiculously large number of lake monsters and sea-serpents that were said to inhabit countless bodies of water around the entire globe.

'Okay,' I said. 'What you're saying does make some sense to me at least; as I've heard things similar to this several times before. But if these things aren't actually physically real animals, then how are they killing people?'

Rob leaned back in the seat and replied matter-of-factly: 'Mind-power: fright, suggestion. They'll stop your heart in a beat with fear. You want someone dead, you kill them through fear; fear of the unknown, fear of anything. That's much better than risking taking someone out with a gun or a knife; there's less of a chance of getting caught.'

'Right; I understand that. But what is so special about this group that it needs so many people dead?'

A big grin came over Rob's face: 'You've hit the nail on the head,' he said, swigging on his drink. 'The group itself doesn't want *anyone* dead.'

'You've lost me,' I replied, utterly puzzled, and proceeded to chug down a big mouthful of alcohol.

Rob continued his convoluted tale and explained further that the Cult of the Moon-Beast was linked with some *very* influential people and that, when needed, the cult was 'hired for its services' – and paid very handsomely, indeed - by the highest echelons of private industry, and even by the Intelligence services of the British Government. As he explained it to me: 'You want someone dead, then you give them a heart-attack by having a monster appearing in their bedroom at night. Or you drive them to suicide by making them think they are going mad if they are seeing werewolves.'

And, as Rob was most keen to remind me, and as I *had* to agree with him, it was an undeniable fact that the sighting of the Man-Monkey in 1879 *was* indeed tied-in *directly* with the story of a man who had apparently then recently drowned in that ominous stretch of the Shropshire Union Canal. Was it possible, I wondered, while musing upon Rob's admittedly very controversial theories, that the man's mind had been so drastically tortured by images of the Man-

Monkey – perhaps brought into our world via the macabre incantations of some unknown individual or group whose identity is now lost to the fog of time, but with similar dark goals to those of the Cult of the Moon-Beast – that he had thrown himself into those dark waters to escape such vile and devilish visions?

Maybe, I thought to myself as I continued in this particular vein that the dead soul at the canal-bridge had engaged in a clandestine, torrid affair with the wife of a local dignitary, who in turn, had secretly hired some infernal wizard to conjure up a paranormal assassin in the vile form of the Man-Monkey to take care of his wife's lover, once and for all.

This scenario sounded *very* much like a story told to me by a man named Colin Perks. An infinitely strange and highly-disturbed character of truly whacked-out proportions, Perks had earnestly asserted that a diabolical winged monster - that he claimed to have personally encountered late one night near the city of Bath - was somehow in league with elements of British intelligence that had themselves stumbled upon a strange, twilight realm populated by a veritable plethora of strange beasts, including the aforementioned winged thing. But what was interesting about Rob's similar story was that at least a part of it seemed to check out – which is far more than can be said for the rambling tales of Colin Perks.

In March 2000, the *Chase Post* newspaper had reported on the story of a 68-year-old Hednesford man who declined to be named, but who claimed to have seen a big cat roaming the Cannock Chase on no less than two occasions. He recalled: 'One Monday lunchtime a few weeks ago I was driving home from Ingestre Park Golf Club when this cat jumped over the hedge then pounced over the ditch. This cat was about 18 to 20 inches high with a long, thick black tail.'

The man proceeded to inform staff at the Golf Club the following day, who responded in what he perceived as being a positively underwhelming fashion: 'I assured the woman I had not been drinking but she didn't seem bothered.' It was two or three weeks later that the man saw the animal – or, at the very least, a similar one – again. This time, it was roughly 6.30 p.m. and it was already getting dark when, while heading for the Golf Club and having just passed the Forestry Commission offices, his headlights picked up something at a distance of about fifty or so yards: 'I saw a pair of green eyes in the hedge. I tooted my horn at it and it ran off.'

Somewhat oddly and intriguingly, he added to the *Chase Post* that: 'Since then I have heard a lot of people are walking with big torches around there. Last Monday I saw about ten people who appeared to be searching for something.'

Precisely what the mysterious, torch-wielding figures were looking for is something that, publicly at least, remains a mystery to this very day. It must be said, however, that if Rob Lea is even remotely correct, then the unnamed man cited in the *Chase Post's* story may very well have stumbled upon the clandestine, late-night activities of the Cult of the Moon-Beast that Rob said were operating in the *exact* same area and in the *exact* same time-frame.

At the time of the meeting, Rob said that there was much more that he could tell me; including precise details of *other* encounters with hairy man-beasts near Ranton and Woodseaves. But, as he worked as a bar-man in a local pub and was due to start his shift in a couple of hours' time, he asked if we could continue the conversation on both another date and at a different locale. I agreed; and Rob said he would telephone me in a day or two. He most assuredly did not, however; and the telephone-number that he had provided to me was completely bogus.

I had to wonder to myself: was Rob nothing more than a deranged fantasist? Or was he simply trying to afford himself a degree of personal protection if things went distinctly awry? Was his name even Rob Lea? Unfortunately, I never uncovered definitive answers to any of those key questions: despite my best attempts to try and locate him, Rob remained completely and utterly elusive; and checks with the many and various pubs, inns, restaurants and hotels in the area utterly failed to identify my shadowy informant or his place of employment. Rob Lea had vanished as mysteriously as had the Man-Monkey on that long-gone January night of 1879.

It must also be stressed that I never did uncover any additional material relative to the alleged Cult of the Moon-Beast that Rob Lea was so obsessed with; and so I still cannot state with absolute certainty that it was not all a creation of the mind of an over-imaginative Rob

Lea. However, I *was* approached by several people - who had also read the *Chase Post* article that had directly led me to meet Rob – and who told me eerie tales of finding dead animals on the Chase that looked suspiciously as if they had been subjected to some sort of ritual slaughter.

One such person was Frank, who, while out walking his dog one day in 1998, had found the remains of five fully-grown foxes laid out in a circle on a patch of grassy ground near the village of Brocton, with the remains of a large, thick candle lying about six or seven feet from the dead bodies. Having no wish at all to get involved in what might very well have turned into a police investigation, Frank quickly grabbed his dog, walked away, and opted not to report his macabre discovery at an official level.

Another account, of a somewhat similar nature at least, surfaced from a couple who had come across a dead deer on the Cannock Chase on a Sunday morning in the late 1970s. Of course, it is a sad, harsh and unfortunate fact of life that deer do get hit, and killed, by cars while racing across the roads of the Cannock Chase from time to time. And this was indeed the first thought of the pair, when they stumbled across the body of the animal on land between the Chase's German Cemetery and what is today called the Pye Green British Telecom Tower.

The deer, I was told, *could* have been hit by a car, and *could* perhaps have dragged itself into the woods before finally taking its last breath – even though the animal had been found at least a couple of hundred yards from the side of the road. However, the most dis-turbing and curious part of the story was the fact that someone, or *something*, had systematically removed the major organs from the animal and had carefully laid them out on the ground in what was most definitely a clear, delineated pattern. Of equal interest to me: the pair added that it looked like the internal organs and body had remained completely untouched by the many other wild animals that live in the woods of the Cannock Chase. Indeed, it was this latter point that most puzzled the couple: why would there be reluctance on the part of the wild creatures of the Cannock Chase to partake in what would most certainly be a considerable and hearty feast?

I had no solid answers for the couple; however, I was always mindful of the fact that, although it certainly could not be considered as definitive proof, it was strange and thought-provoking reports such as these that led me to strongly suspect that Rob Lea was quite possibly telling me the truth all along about the ritualistic and sacrificial after-dark activities of the Cult of the Moon-Beast. And he did, of course, have the photographs from his father's farm, too. And there was one final tale that reached me of animal mutilation that instantly snapped my mind back to the days of my initial informant in this odd saga: Fletcher.

In this case, the confidante was actually a still-serving member of the Staffordshire Constabulary who had quietly investigated the mutilation and killing of several ducks and other water-birds at none other than Shugborough Hall a few years earlier. Again, there were veiled allusions to black magic, witchcraft and dark, occult practices being rife throughout the woods of the Cannock Chase after the sun had set; although nothing was ever proven to any firm degree. However, it seemed to me that wherever and whenever hairy man-beasts could be found, ancient rites and dark, archaic rituals seemed never to be far behind.

CHAPTER VII
THE ENCOUNTERS CONTINUE

Simon was yet another character that popped out of the crypto-zoological woodwork in the wake of the article on the Man-Monkey that Irene Bott and I had written for the *Chase Post* in the summer of 2000, and who I met for drinks one evening at an old pub in the Staffordshire city of Lichfield. A jovial, anorak-and-green-welly-wearing Bill Oddie-style bird-watcher and nature-lover, Simon had told me in an initial and brief telephone call that he had been strolling by the Shropshire Union Canal, approximately three-quarters of a mile from Bridge 39, on a bright summer's day in 1982 when he heard what he described as 'a really loud noise from across the other side of the canal and in the trees'.

Notably, Simon added to me that: 'It was like [the scream of] a fox and I thought that's what it was.' That is until, as he described it, 'I saw this bloody great thing, like a gorilla, stand up [and] take off. I thought: bugger me, what's that? But it was gone before I could think to do anything else about it. And, in any case, it was the other side of the canal and I was nowhere near a bridge to get over there. But I shook after, I'll tell you.'

Well, after hearing those brief - yet most certainly remarkable - details I definitely could not let things rest there; and so after greetings were exchanged at the pub, I ordered us a round of lager, a plate of food, and dug deeper into the strange saga of Simon, who went on to relate to me that at the time of the encounter he was twenty-three years of age and was then situated at a well-known West Midlands-based college, where he was studying for a degree in zoology. And as he became more relaxed about talking with me, Simon divulged that he had a, ahem, covert agenda for his trek to the dark canal: he had a girl with him that shared his passion for ornithology; and, as a result, he was most keen to try and cement a little bit of action of the bird kind for *himself* in the quiet confines of the tree-shrouded canal.

That action, however, never came to pass: Simon said that although they remained friends – 'and only friends, unfortunately', he added - he had never spoken to the girl again after 1984 (the year in which he finished his college education), and he seriously doubted that she would speak to me anyway, taking into consideration her over-whelmingly hysterical state after the encounter. Fortunately, Simon himself had no such qualms about staying silent.

Simon's sighting had lasted only a few, scant seconds; and so I was therefore forced to try and glean as much data as possible from what was a distinctly brief encounter. According to Simon, he and the girl were walking along the bank of the canal, chatting and laughing, when the welcome and relaxed atmosphere was utterly destroyed by two specific things: the startling sight of dozens of birds fleeing the area while frantically chirping loudly in the process, and a sudden, strange screaming noise that enveloped the entire area.

Simon told me that it didn't take a genius at all to work out where the noise was coming from: 'It was right opposite us, mate; right across the cut.' Stressing to me, again, that his initial thought was that the scream was that of a fox, Simon was horrified when out of the bushes reared a man-like figure that was covered with glossy, dark hair across its entire body and head. 'Only the face and hands didn't have hair,' he explained to me, adding that the creature looked 'strong' and appeared to use the weight of one arm to 'launch itself off the ground and out [of] the bushes' and into the safety and camouflage of the surrounding woods.

In answer to my questions, Simon said that the creature was not at all of the extreme height attributed to such cryptozoological entities as the Yeti of the Himalayas and the Bigfoot of North America, but was perhaps five to five-and-a-half feet in stature at the *very* most (and possibly slightly less, even). And it appeared to be both highly agile and very muscular, and certainly not the sort of beast that a person would want to cross paths with on either a dark, winter's night in 1879, or on a bright, summer's day in 1982. In essence, that was almost it. And, I was highly impressed by Simon's character, his matter-of-fact style of relating the account, the fact that he did not seek to speculate on his memorable encounter, and that he stuck only to the data that he could still personally recall – bizarre and controversial as it most assuredly was.

But there was one final thing that Simon had to say to me that was profoundly eerie, to say the very least, and that instantly struck a chord and made me think back to the claims of Rob Lea concerning the Cult of the Moon Beast. Simon duly expanded: 'I say this thing looked like a gorilla because that's the closest thing that I can think of. But it looked like a gorilla directly face-on. But when it turned sideways and ran off I could see when it was side-on that it had a muzzle; a very long muzzle. I hate to say this because I know how it sounds: but side-on it looked just like a werewolf; even with long flattened ears like a dog on the side of its head.'

Was it possible that the Man-Monkey was not some form of ape-like entity, after all; but in reality was nothing less than a shape-shifting lycanthrope? Or was it some weird chimera that possessed the unique attributes of several beasts? Certainly, Britain had a rich history of werewolf-style encounters: there was, for example, the werewolf of Flixton; the Abbotsham werewolf; the strange saga of the Hexham Heads; as well as countless other report suggesting that diabolical lycanthropes were secretly walking the ancient pathways and dense woods and forests of Britain. Simon and I joked about how such things were 'paws for thought', swilled down the remains of our drinks, and headed off into the night.

For me, it was a journey home-bound, and one that (after making a detour to visit a friend in nearby Etchinghill) took me once again through the thick and ominous woods of the Cannock Chase. I recall keeping a close watch on those same woods as I negotiated their long and winding roads. Just in case…

'Florrie' Abbott grew up not far from the village Woodseaves, and, at the age of eighty-two, still distinctly remembered hearing uncanny tales of the Man-Monkey as a child in the late 1920s. Interestingly, according to Florrie, one such tale that had been diligently passed down through her family told of a supernatural-like encounter with the Man-Monkey in the village of Ranton – only a short journey from Woodseaves - in 1848: which was, notably, more than *thirty years* before the story chronicled by Charlotte S. Burne within the pages of *Shropshire Folklore* even surfaced.

As the story was related to me by an amusingly cantankerous Florrie (whose daughter was chiefly responsible for acting as the go-between that brought us together after the *Chase Post* highlighted my tale of the Man-Monkey), it was an autumn night in 1848 when the witness – a young girl on Florrie's father's side of the family who was walking to her parents home in Ranton – encountered in the shadows of the neighbouring property a five-foot-tall, man-like creature that was covered in dark, matted hair and that emitted strange grunting noises. For more than a minute or two, the pair stood staring at each other, both seemingly transfixed. Suddenly, said Florrie, the animal – if that is what it truly was – ambled off towards a nearby field and promptly vanished, quite literally, in a bright flash of light.

In the Abbott household, it seems that the Man-Monkey was akin to being the local equivalent of the classic bogeyman, as Florrie well recalled: 'My brother and sister and I were all told this story as children and that if we were mischievous the Man-Monkey would come for us. The story was well-known in our family when I was a little girl.'

Another story that surfaced to me in 2000 and that most definitely deserves a mention came from a man who declined a personal meeting with me and even declined to reveal his name; but who, in a lunchtime telephone-call, briefly told me how he had personally heard of an encounter with the beast of the bridge at the height of the Second World War. According to the tale, the man was a twelve-year-old in 1943 when a young evacuee - a boy of about nine or ten who hailed from somewhere in London - came to stay with his immediate neighbours.

The pair would regularly play in the woods and fields around Woodseaves during the summer of that year, and had jolly japes and adventures of a kind that would make even the *Secret Seven* envious. However, a degree of dark melancholy overcame the young Londoner, when he confided in my caller that - one night - he had overheard the husband and wife he was staying with quietly discussing a strange event that had occurred several days earlier: namely the sighting by the husband of a large, hair-covered thing 'like an upright bear' that had been seen walking menacingly through Woodseaves shortly after midnight.

The witness had apparently been deeply disturbed by the encounter and swore his wife to complete and utter secrecy. My source knew no more than that, and had not spoken to the boy from London for more than half a century; however - for what it was worth - he said that he wanted to relate the details to me, as he thought I would find them interesting. I most certainly did! I thanked the man and he quickly hung up the telephone; never to call again.

Interestingly, as I knew very well, sightings of mysterious bear-like animals were not exactly unknown within the confines of the Britain Isles. Indeed, the researcher Jan Williams had written about close encounters with such specific entities in darkest Oxfordshire in both 1993 and 1994. In her own words:

> The ancient forest of Wychwood, straddling the border of Oxfordshire and Gloucestershire, was once a favourite hunting ground of kings. In the nineteenth century it was a wild and lawless place, the haunt of highwaymen, Black Dogs, and the dreaded Snow Foresters - strange spirits whose howls and screams could be heard echoing through winter nights, and which were known to attack snowbound travellers. Remnants of the ancient woodland still exist along the valley of the Evelode. Despite its proximity to the busy modern city of Oxford and the tourist traps of the Cotswolds, Wychwood remains a secret forest, a refuge for fox, badger and deer, and a memory of Old England.
>
> Residents of Charlbury, within the forest bounds, have taken a light-hearted view of reports of a bear roaming the woods. The village baker sold 'Buns to feed the Bear', the butcher displayed 'Bear steaks' in his window, and local publicans played host to bear-suited regulars.
>
> Charlbury's previous claim to cryptozoological fame lay with 'Skippy', an escaped wallaby which bounded around the village for a few months in 1985. Wallabies are becoming commonplace in England, but the wolf which killed fourteen sheep in 1935 was more of a rarity. An escapee from Oxford Zoo at Kidlington, it was tracked down by a photographer from the *Oxford Mail*. Face to face with the wolf, he decided that discretion was the better part of valour and shot it with gun rather than camera.
>
> Whilst many villagers are sceptical of the bear, Mr. Waring, landlord of 'The Bull' at Charlbury, is keeping an open-mind. He has tracked bears in Canada, and believes a bear could easily survive in the area. 'It is the right sort of terrain, and there is plenty of food in the woods.' And he has found large and unusual prints in the woods, though sadly these were too distorted for a definite identification.
>
> The main witness is John Blackwell, who runs a mixed farm

at Dean and keeps a variety of livestock. In September 1992, Mr. Blackwell saw an unusual animal near his 21-acre wood. Remembering 'Skippy', his first thought was of a wallaby 'with its tail chopped off', but closer sightings on the following two nights convinced him that it was a bear. The animal was the size of an Old English Sheep-dog, with small pointed ears, massive, great hocks', and no tail. Its thick fur was a dark rusty-brown, with lighter sandy-brown patches on belly and flanks. The ears were held down, and it walked on all fours with a pronounced 'waddling' motion.

The 'bear' was not seen again for several months, but there were indications that something strange was living in the woods. Huge prints were found on the land, the farm dogs barked continually in the area of a thickly overgrown bank, and two fish ponds on the farm were visited by some large animal which left a trail of smashed and flattened rushes. On one occasion cows on the farm were so badly frightened that they refused to eat for five days.

In late May 1993, Mr. Blackwell heard a strange hooting noise from the wood. He walked towards the sound, thinking at first that it was a cockerel crowing, but as he got nearer it changed to a continuous howl. Two fallow deer were grazing on the woodland edge. As they moved off, the bear-like animal came out of the trees, following them at a run. It left huge prints, which Mrs. Blackwell measured against her size 9 Wellingtons. The prints were larger and showed long claws. On the following day the animal appeared again. It was lying in long grass and put its head up as the farmer approached. The farmer says none of his livestock have been attacked and the animal seems curious rather than aggressive towards people. He felt it should be left alone, and only came forward when other reports appeared in the press.

In January [of 1994] bus-driver Greg Gilbert and passenger Sarah Cooper saw a reddish-brown animal walk across the Charlbury road. In contrast to Mr. Blackwell's sightings, the creature walked upright, on its hind legs. Another witness, James Graham-Cloete, of Chadlington, stated he had seen it standing by the roadside. A spokesman for the nearby Cotswold Wildlife Park was dismissive. He suggested witnesses were seeing a badger. But John Blackwell is a traditional farmer with an interest in wildlife, who sits up at night and watches badgers. A bear in Oxfordshire may seem unlikely, but is it any more likely that a man who has been watching badgers for twenty years should suddenly mistake one for an exotic animal?

Press reports of unusual animals often encourage other witnesses to come forward, and it seems the 'bear' is not the only strange creature roaming Wychwood. Earlier this year, Mrs. Nicky Sherbook, of Taston, near Dean, was surprised to find one of her sheep killed and half-eaten. She said it had been 'ripped to shreds'. Shortly afterwards, Mrs. Sherbrook's seventeen-tear-old son, Harry, was walking with a friend in a field bordering onto woodland when they disturbed a fox-sized animal. It was a light silvery colour, with a black stripe down the spine, a flat cat-like head, and a big bushy tail. It ran very quickly down the field and into the woods, passing a third boy who dashed up to ask the others what it was. All three teenagers are used to foxes, and were quite certain it was not one.

It looks as though Oxfordshire's 'secret forest' is harbouring cryptic creatures - or was that a Snow Forester howling in the woods?

The tale of the mystery bear of Wychwood was never resolved; however, for me there was still much more to come. Indeed, the most controversial story of all that I received during this specific period came from Danny Thomas, a thirty-year-old Scot, then living in Aberdeen, and who I drove up to meet personally shortly before Christmas 2000.

CHAPTER VIII
DISASTER AT THE BRIDGE

With a chapter-name like that, you, the reader, might be forgiven for naturally assuming that something of truly catastrophic proportions occurred at the infamous canal bridge near Woodseaves at some point in its dark and ominous history. However, you would be wrong; *very* wrong, in fact. The bridge that I wish to bring to your attention right now is located a good many miles from that which has been the subject of so much debate and intrigue thus far. Yet, according to the aforementioned Danny Thomas, at least, the bridge with which he has such an overriding and dark obsession *is* inextricably linked with the one situated deep in the heart of central England.

Danny, who bore more than a passing resemblance to *Clash* bass-guitarist Paul Simonon, lived with two friends named Paul and Strachan in a small, cramped flat above a downtown fish-and-chip shop, and had an overriding interest (and a truly unfathomable interest, at that, for someone of his age) in the 1970s band *Bread*. And, as we sat and ate a fine fish supper purchased from the good people of Greek stock who worked one floor down, he told me his eerie story.

According to Danny, on a particular evening in January 1879, his great-great-grandfather, who had apparently suffered from some form of severe mental affliction, had committed suicide by hurling himself off of Scotland's Tay Bridge, and right into the harsh depths of Dundee's Firth of Tay. Of course, the date of the suicide – January 1879 – immediately jumped out at me as being the exact same time-frame in which the Man-Monkey had been seen prowling around the countryside near the village of Woodseaves. But there was much more to come: namely that in the immediate days that followed the family's tragic loss, ominous reports began to quietly circulate within the close-knit confines of the neighbourhood of a shaggy-haired man-beast that was seen roaming the bridge late at night, and that came to be known locally as the 'Shuggy'. And, indeed, the fact that – as with the encounter at Woodseaves – the drowning at the Tay Bridge had also been followed by sightings of a strange, hairy entity hardly went amiss in these quarters, either.

This was all very interesting to me, and I commented as much to Danny: here were two cases, at bridges in vastly different parts of the British Isles, that both involved human deaths and man-beast en-counters . Danny was far from finished, however, and he drew my attention to a tragic disaster of truly epic proportions that had oc-curred at the same Tay Bridge in December 1879, eleven months after the unfortunate death of his great-great-grandfather.

The known facts, at least, were relatively straightforward: almost two miles in length and carrying a single rail track, the bridge – com-pleted in February 1878 to the plans of Sir Thomas Bouch – was the longest in the world at that time. Proposals for such a bridge dated back to 1854; and its foundation stone had been laid with ceremony on July 22, 1871. The first engine duly crossed the bridge on Septem-ber 22, 1877, and the bridge was officially opened by Queen Victoria on June 1, 1878. Ulysses S. Grant worded it correctly when he com-mented that it was 'a big bridge for a small city'. But that situation would soon change – and most definitely not for the better.

It was an appropriately dark and stormy night on December 28, 1879 when, at around 7.15 p.m., and as a veritable storm of truly deluge-style proportions was blowing right down the length of the estuary, the central navigation spans of the Tay Bridge collapsed and plum-meted into the Firth of Tay – taking with them a train and six car-riages that resulted in no less than seventy-five untimely and tragic deaths. Legend and urban-myth that still circulates in Dundee to this very day holds that - had illness not intervened - none other than Karl Marx himself would have been aboard the doomed train.

A Court of Inquiry set up at the time decided that: '…the fall of the bridge was occasioned by the insufficiency of the cross bracing and its fastenings to sustain the force of the gale'. Had the wind-bracing been properly concluded, said the Court, the bridge might very well have withstood the intense battering of the mighty storm. Regardless of the real nature of the tragedy, however, the trail of death was still far from over. Plans were duly made for a new bridge to be built – according to the designs of one William Henry Barlow. The first stone was laid on July 6, 1883; and, by the time of its completion, no less than fourteen of the construction workers were dead, all from a variety of accidents.

It must be said that Danny Thomas was not an adherent of the theory that the Tay Bridge disaster could be attributed to something as down-to-earth as the stormy and relentless British weather. No: it was his firm belief that the dark and sinister forces of the Shuggy were at work on that most tragic of all nights. As we continued to munch on our fish-and-chips and drink copious amounts of *Tennents Super* lager, Danny related to me a story that eerily paralleled that of the infamous Mothman of the United States.

There can be few people reading this book who have not at least heard of the legendary Mothman of Point Pleasant, Virginia, who so terrorised the area between November 1966 and December 1967. A diabolical, winged entity with glowing, red eyes, Mothman's appearance intriguingly coincided with a plethora of UFO encounters, confrontations with Men in Black, and a whole range of Fortean weirdness of a truly dizzying variety – all of which elected to descend upon the unfortunate city, and people, of Point Pleasant. And the strange events came to a climax on December 15, 1967, when the city's Silver Bridge (so named after its aluminium paint) that spanned the Ohio River and connected Point Pleasant to Gallipolis, Ohio, collapsed into the river, tragically claiming forty-six lives.

And while a down-to-earth explanation most certainly circulated – that a flaw in a single eye-bar in a suspension chain was the chief culprit – many saw, and still continue to see to this very day, the cause as being directly linked with the ominous and brooding presence of the accursed Mothman.

As will also be apparent to most of the good readers of this book, Mothman has its British winged-counterparts – such as the foul Owlman of Mawnan Church, Cornwall; the monstrous, winged gargoyle of Glastonbury that protects, some say at least, the final resting place of King Arthur and his legendary knights; and the huge, bat-like beast seen at Sandling Park, Hythe, Kent by a group of teenagers on a fateful night in 1963.

And, certainly, several of those that allegedly crossed paths with the

Owlman of Cornwall and the Gargoyle of Glastonbury suffered nothing but complete and utter misfortune and bad luck until they took determined steps to back away from the heart of the mystery. And Danny was a firm believer that the presence of the Shuggy at the Tay Bridge was the cause of equal bad luck and disaster.

It was his overwhelming belief that the precise cause of the Tay Bridge disaster of December 1879 was his great-great-grandfather: returned, after death, to our plane of existence in the spectral form of some vile man-beast that haunted the darkened corners of the bridge – positively oozing negative energy and creating an atmosphere of death, doom, tragedy and decay as it did so.

Danny possessed the hollow eyes of a man with a lot of dark and troubling secrets, and the mind of someone that was both tortured and frightened. It was Danny's belief that suicide results in a restless, insane soul that is destined to wreak havoc wherever it may roam; and that prime examples of this could be seen in the 1879 events that followed the deaths by drowning of his long-gone relative at Tay Bridge, and of the unnamed man at Woodseaves. And, in his own mind, Danny had a very good reason to be frightened: twice he had attempted suicide – once at the age of seventeen and then again shortly before his twenty-third birthday.

It must be said that from what Danny had to say, the seemingly half-hearted attempts to end his life were more like classic cries-for-help than anything more serious. Yet, he told me quietly, he feared that one day complete and utter blackness and depression would descend upon him, and he would indeed take his own life – at the Tay Bridge, no less. Danny's overriding fear was that his soul, too, would be eternally damned; and that, like his great-great-grandfather, he would return to our world in some vile hairy guise, forever destined to wildly spread misery and death by both moonlight and a stormy wind atop Dundee's Tay Bridge.

And it was at that point I realised Danny had not invited me up to his Scottish home to discuss his theories as such, but rather to offer me a dire warning. While the following is not an exact quote, and is instead merely based upon my own hastily scrawled notes taken at the time, it *is* a pretty close approximation of Danny's final words to me as I left his home for the long car journey back to central England:

'Stop digging into the Man-Monkey: it's going to get into you and follow you – wherever you go. You'll end up followed, possessed, eaten up by it all. That's what it does: it thrives on hate and death and will manipulate you to get what it wants. That's the fate of suicides: they come back; but not as we expect them to. Suicides go to hell; their souls then belong to the Devil, and he then sends them out to make death.'

I nodded, unsure if I was listening to the ravings of a deranged madman or the dark truths of an enlightened visionary. Danny's last words for me as we said our goodbyes were: 'Let it drop.' I have to say that I mused upon those final three words from Danny for months afterwards.

*The infamous Bridge 39 on the Shropshire Union Canal,
home of the macabre Man-Monkey.*

*Since at least 1879, sightings of a hairy monkey-like creature
have been reported from within the woods that surround Bridge 39.*

It was on this particular stretch of the Shropshire Union Canal that the Man-Monkey was seen by two witnesses in the summer of 1982.

The only life-forms that Nick Redfern personally ever saw on the Shropshire Union Canal were a family of ducks!

*During the hot summer of 1976, both a large hairy animal and a
giant eel-like creature were allegedly witnessed by a man fishing in the canal.*

*The road-bridge that crosses the Shropshire Union Canal, where the
Man-Monkey attacked a terrified soul in January 1879.*

Late one night in the early 1970s, lorry-driver Bob Carroll saw the Man-Monkey at close quarters as it bounded across the road-bridge and down towards the canal.

A distinctly Man-Monkey-like encounter occurred near Chartley Castle, Staffordshire in 1986. The witnesses had just attended Abbots Bromley's famous and historic Horn Dance.

Twenty years after the Man-Monkey was seen near Chartley Castle, a large and complex Crop Circle formation appeared on farm-land adjacent to the castle.

A second image of the 2006 Crop Circle near Chartley Castle.

While investigating the 2006 Crop Circle adjacent to Chartley Castle,
Nick Redfern found a pile of peacock feathers lying on the ground.
What this means, he hasn't the foggiest!

In 1995, Jackie Houghton encountered a large, lumbering Man-Monkey-style beast on this stretch of road that crosses Staffordshire's Cannock Chase woods.

On more than one occasion, dead animals - allegedly sacrificed for use in archaic rites and rituals to summon up the Man-Monkey - were found in the vicinity of the Cannock Chase's Pye Green Tower.

Cannock Chase - the home of a monstrous spectral ape?

Picture courtesy of Jonathan Downes/ CFZ

The German cemetery on Cannock Chase
where several Man-Monkey encounters have taken place.

Picture courtesy of Jonathan Downes/ CFZ

Shugborough Hall, Staffordshire, the alleged site of a 1981
Man-Monkey-style encounter.

Stories abound that the Man-Monkey was seen in the grounds
of Shugborough Hall at some point in the 1960s.

Nick Redfern (left in the photo) stands atop a bridge at Shugborough Hall, where the Man-Monkey was seen in 1981.

The stretch of water at Shugborough Hall, where the Man-Monkey vanished in 1981.

Geoff Lincoln in Bolam Woods.

Picture courtesy of Jonathan Downes/ CFZ

The walkway in Bolam woods where witnesses encountered a `Yeti` in early 2003.

Picture courtesy of Jonathan Downes/ CFZ

The woods where Jon Downes had his sighting.

Picture courtesy of Jonathan Downes/ CFZ

Bolam Woods in January 2003.

Picture courtesy of Jonathan Downes/ CFZ

Scotland's Tay Bridge, which was the site of a fatal rail disaster in 1879, was also reputedly the domain of a wild, hairy creature that came to be known as the Shuggy.

Athelhampton Hall, near Dorchester, Dorset, most famous ghost is that of the Martyn family's pet ape. It is said that the animal can be heard scratching behind the panelling in the Great Chamber where it is trapped in a secret staircase.

Picture courtesy of Mark North/ wwwdarkdorset.co.uk

'He who looks at Martyn's ape,
Martyn's ape shall look at him'.

Picture courtesy of Mark North/ wwwdarkdorset.co.uk

The legend of the Hairy Hands takes place on the B3212 road between Postbridge and Two Bridges, Dartmoor.

An ape –like creature haunts the ruins of Dundonald Castle .

CHAPTER IX
A CLOSE ENCOUNTER OF
THE HAIRY KIND

Certainly, one of the most fascinating reports that surfaced in the summer of 2000 came from a man named Bob Carroll who lived on the East Anglian coast. However, such was my insanely hectic schedule that a personal, face-to-face meeting with Bob had to wait until the very end of December, when I was then due to travel to Rendlesham Forest, Suffolk with former U.S. Air Force man Larry Warren to commemorate the 20th anniversary of the infamous UFO landing of December 1980. And so it was that twenty-four hours after roaming the woods with Larry and a group of lads from the *Hull UFO Society*, I was about to interview a man who claimed to have seen the Man-Monkey for himself in the early 1970s – and at the site of the infamous canal bridge, no less.

My grandparents on my mother's side of the family were from the historic city of Norwich and my mother lived right in the heart of the city until 1955, when, at the age of eighteen, she married my father - having met him while he was stationed in East Anglia with the Royal Air Force in the early 1950s. And, as my grandparents continued to live in Norwich right up until the time of their deaths, the sprawling city, its rich folklore and the glorious landscape and majesty of East Anglia were very familiar and welcome territories to me. Needless to say, I heartily relished the idea of a mini-road-trip to the East-Coast and to some of my favourite old haunts. As per usual on such treks, I loaded the car with snacks, sandwiches, cold drinks, a flask of tea, spare clothes, and ensured that the radio was tuned in to *Virgin*.

It was late at night when I arrived at Bob Carroll's delightful, old stone house that was situated near a steep drop that overlooked a harsh and windswept North Sea. The utter lack of light-pollution firmly ensured that the entire area was enveloped in darkness, and the crashing of the waves below was my only real indication at that time of night, that the uncaring, cold seas beckoned only a few hundred yards away.

I duly knocked on the old wooden door, and was quickly greeted by a large, robust man sporting a full white beard and a bright red face. He was dressed in jeans and a heavy, brown jumper; he looked like Father Christmas, and sounded like Brian Blessed. He shook my hand vigorously, and invited me in. The very first thing that happened was that Bob headed over to the fridge, whereupon he flung open its door, and pulled out – and duly thrust into my hand - a jug (and I *do* mean a jug) of homemade cider. And sitting on his kitchen table was a plate of thick, cheese and Branston Pickle sandwiches that he had thoughtfully prepared in advance, and by way of a fine midnight feast.

As it transpired, the liquid refreshment and food were both very welcome, since we chatted until what was easily three o'clock in the morning – and all to the background tunes of some folk group, comprised of sweater-wearing, acoustic-guitar-players from the Isle of Man (or somewhere, at least – the Isle of Man imagery merely seems appropriate to me), who performed truly cringe-inducing songs about stone circles, Cornish tin mines, and little Welsh villages. But that was okay: Bob was quick to tell me what he thought of punk rock (not a lot, unsurprisingly); and we both laughed heartily – agreeing that the world would be a *very* boring place if everyone was of a like mind when it came to music.

It transpired that a distinctly synchronistic series of events had led Bob to contact me. Although he originally hailed from the majestic Midlands (well, *I* consider the Midlands to be majestic – to a degree, anyway), he had retired early to East Anglia in 1981. However, Bob's sister lived in the Staffordshire locale of Armitage and she had telephoned him after reading the article on the Man-Monkey that had appeared in the *Chase Post*.

Notably, Bob's sister would later tell me that she hardly ever saw the *Chase Post*; and it was only down to pure chance – while meeting a friend in Cannock for lunch one day – that she picked up a copy of the relevant issue of the newspaper that happened to include my *C-Files* story on the Man-Monkey. Bob said to me that he had thought long and hard about whether or not to contact me; but ultimately decided to go ahead and take the plunge. I was certainly most glad that he did. Indeed, Bob's sister had a very good and relevant reason for contacting him about the article.

As I sat back and listened to what he had to say, Bob told me that from the age of twenty-five until his late forties he had worked as a lorry-driver – and in the period from 1970 to 1977 specifically for a well-known paint manufacturing company. Somewhat ironically and interestingly, the division of the company that employed Bob all those years ago made regular deliveries to the head-office of the paint-and-wallpaper distribution company I had worked at as a van-driver in the 1980s.

Bob was very keen to stress to me that, aside from that which he was about to tell me, he had never experienced any other type of paranormal event in his entire life; and after his retirement and his wife's unfortunate death in 1997, he was focused on but four things: his love of the sea; his newly-acquired terrier puppy, Jack; his British folk music CDs; and his huge collection of model boats, ships and galleons that adorned the shelves of his cottage. But he had never forgotten the events of the early 1970s that so dominated his mind throughout our after-dark conversation.

Bob was unable to recall the exact date of the incident at issue; but he was pretty sure that it was either January or February of either 1972 or 1973. It was the early hours of the morning, at any rate, and he was driving to a spot where he was due to make a 6.00 a.m. delivery, having picked up a pallet of paint from a depot in Leicester that same evening. Everything was completely normal until he approached that damned bridge. Stressing that 'it was all over in a few seconds', Bob said that it was his natural instinct to slow down as he reached the bridge; and, as he did so, he was shocked to see from his cab 'a hairy man come storming through the trees and vanish down to the canal'.

Bob was both surprised and amazed by the incredible speed and apparent agility of the beast as it bounded across the road, and was subsequently and quickly lost to sight. He estimated that its height was four-and-a-half to five-feet at the very most, and that it looked 'well built', and was covered in what looked like black-blue coloured hair or fur. He did concede, however, that: 'Maybe that blue tinge was from the headlights though; it's hard to say.' Stressing that he had 'always been a gung-ho type', Bob pulled over to the side of the road, quickly turned on the hazard-lights of his lorry, and ran 'full belt' back to the scene of his bizarre experience.

'I was bloody daft,' he told me, with hindsight, 'because I say that I pulled over; but, really I was practically just stopped in the lane. If anyone had come along speeding around those bends there would have been a hell of an accident.'

On reaching the canal bridge, he quickly peered over both sides; however, the total lack of light and the utter darkness made any attempt to see anything tangible nigh-on impossible. But there was one other odd thing that Bob was keen to tell me: 'The only thing that did happen at the bridge was that from pretty close by I heard a noise while I was looking over the bridge. If you asked me to describe it – and my sister will verify to you that I said the same to her years ago – I would say it was like a baby crying. But it sounded a lot louder, and like it was evil or not right; and [I] got a funny feeling hearing it.'

And while it may not, perhaps, have a direct bearing upon the remarkable encounter, Bob told me that when he returned to his vehicle: 'It was like the battery was flat for a minute or two, then it kicked in.' As I knew and as will become graphically apparent later, such puzzling problems with mechanical and electrical equipment were staple parts of certain man-beast encounters. Bob related to me that he continued on his journey and told no-one of the details of the strange events in question until the late 1970s when he watched an episode of the old *In Search Of...* series narrated by Leonard 'Mr. Spock' Nimoy, and then duly – and quietly - confided in his wife, his sister and her now-deceased husband.

Bob and I chatted for several long hours about the nature of the beast and what it may or may not have been. But, to his lasting credit, Bob never tried to elaborate upon his noteworthy tale, and he did not attempt to spice it up in any fashion, whatsoever. I concluded that here was a man who had simply seen something strange and who was keen to relate the facts to me in the hope of securing some firm answers. Unfortunately, I had no answers to give him.

I stayed with Bob for another day and evening and he treated me to a delicious home-cooked stew that ensured I was firmly fuelled for a late-night drive to the village of Corsham, Wiltshire, where I was due to meet a former Royal Air Force man who claimed to know dark and disturbing secrets about clandestine RAF investigations of unidentified flying objects undertaken back in the early-to-mid 1960s. But since that had absolutely nothing whatsoever to do with the Man-Monkey of Bridge 39, I will refrain from saying any more.

What I *will* say, however, is that as 2000 came to an end and a new year began, I was faced with *another* lead that I was determined to resolve – and it was one that focused on a man named Paul Bell, whose story of an encounter with the Man-Monkey was surely one of the most unusual of all.

CHAPTER X
THE MONKEY AND THE
SERPENT

The remarkable tale of Paul Bell is, for me at least, a highly memorable one. As was the case with a number of the people I had spoken with during the course of my investigations of the Man-Monkey legend, Bell provided a story that was fascinating to listen to, extremely provocative in nature, but utterly – and unfortunately - impossible to prove with any degree of absolute certainty. And the controversial fact that he claimed to have seen not one, but *two*, wildly different creatures of a distinctly cryptozoological nature near Bridge 39 on the Shropshire Union Canal way back in the hot summer of 1976, only added to the complexity of the puzzle.

As with practically all of my interviews of a Man-Monkey nature, the one with Bell was undertaken in a pub – namely Pelsall's *Old House at Home*, a place where - as a teenager - I sometimes hung out with my mates, when, under the fascist regime of then Prime Minister Margaret Thatcher, we were all briefly broke and on the dole. Bell had telephoned me a few days after New Year's Day 2001, and proceeded to inform me that he had read some of my articles on unexplained phenomena that had appeared in the *Chase Post*, as well as other features penned by me and that had been published in a short-lived Solihull-based newspaper called *The Planet on Sunday* that I wrote for from late 1999 to early 2000, before - after eight issues - it summarily folded, and vanished into total oblivion. And, learning that I lived locally – he resided in the relatively nearby town of Stourbridge – Bell phoned me one morning asking if we could 'have a chat'.

Well, I often get such unexpected telephone calls out of the blue, and so there was nothing particularly unusual about that at all. And receiving a telephone call specifically about the Man-Monkey wasn't that out-of-the-ordinary either, given the fact that I had written about the hairy beast in local newspapers on several occasions by now, and had regularly discussed the affair at length on radio stations across the West Midlands and Staffordshire for the previous six or seven months.

But it's certainly not every day that you get a telephone call from someone saying that they had seen both a large, monkey-like animal and a giant eel (or possibly a large snake) at Bridge 39 – which is precisely what Bell was earnestly claiming to have encountered almost a quarter of a century earlier. Wondering if this was all just a genial (or malicious, even) wind-up, I elected not to waste petrol on what might have turned out to be nothing more than a fruitless drive to Stourbridge; and so, instead, I told Bell that he would have to come to me. Without any hesitation whatsoever, he agreed, and thus plans were formulated to meet on January 16 in the bar of the aforementioned *Old House at Home* pub.

Unlike some of the people that I have met in my twenty years as a Fortean, there was absolutely nothing even remotely weird at all about Paul Bell: he was genial, in his mid-fifties, and arrived wearing a *Wolverhampton Wanderers* t-shirt, track-suit trousers, and white trainers. We sat and had a couple of pints of lager and chatted about this and that for a while (including his idols, football legends Brian Clough and Bill Shankley), and then finally got down to the business at hand: namely, the crux of his remarkable tale.

Bell said that he was a keen fisherman, and told me how in July and August 1976 – a time that I remember very well, as we moved house that summer and I made the big change from junior school to Pelsall's *Grange Hill*-like Comprehensive School – he had spent several Saturdays out at the canal with his rods, reels, bait, and his cans of Watney's Red and favourite beef-and-onion sandwiches; soaking in the intense heat of what was without doubt an absolutely scalding hot couple of months. Indeed, I seriously doubt that anyone who is old enough to remember the summer of seventy-six will ever quite forget those truly extraordinary temperatures that briefly and memorably plunged the entire nation into complete and utter scalding chaos. But it was far stranger things than the occasional extreme nature of the British weather that Paul Bell had fixed on his mind.

He told me how, on one particular Saturday afternoon. he was sat near the water's edge on a small wooden stool that he always carried with him, when he was 'literally frozen solid' by the sight of 'what at first I thought was a big log floating down the cut, about sixty or seventy feet away'. According to Bell, however, it was no log: it was something else entirely. Indeed, as it got closer, Bell was both astonished and horrified to see a large 'dark brown and black coloured' eel or snake-like creature – possibly ten feet in length or a little bit more – moving slowly in the water, with its head – that 'looked like a black sheep' -flicking rapidly from side to side.

Although he had an old Polaroid camera with him, said Bell, he never even thought to take a photograph; and instead merely stared in both awe and shock as the animal cruised leisurely and blissfully past him, before finally vanishing out of sight. Bell stressed that the creature apparently did not see him ('or if it did, it never attacked me'), and did not appear to exhibit any outright hostile tendencies.

Well, this was all very interesting to me for one, key reason: I had actually heard, on at least three previous occasions, other note-worthy stories of distinctly large eels that had allegedly been sighted in the winding canals of Birmingham and certain areas of Staffordshire from the 1970s onwards. So, in other words, Bell's story was not *that* wild, after all.

One particularly memorable account originated with a lorry-driver who recalled such a sighting somewhere in Birmingham in the late 1980s; and that 'shook the staff rigid' at a plumber's merchants that overlooked the stretch of canal in question. In this case, the animal was described as being dark brown in colour and was said to be no less than an astonishing fifteen feet in length. Supposedly, it had been briefly seen by a fork-lift driver, who had sat, not surprisingly mesmerised, watching it 'circling' one particular area of the canal frequented by a large number of semi-tame ducks that the staff at the plumber's merchant would regularly feed with bread during their daily lunch-hour.

But more intriguing was the story of Norman Dodd, who had lived for many years in Scotland and who, in the 1970s, regularly commuted to the Midlands on business. It was *also* at some point in the hot summer of 1976 that he, too had a remarkable encounter - on the Cannock Chase, no less, with what he stated firmly was either a large snake or eel. Unfortunately, when I personally interviewed Dodd in 1995, he could not recall the exact location where the incident had taken place, but he *was* able to state with certainty that it was a small pool – no more than twenty feet by thirty feet in size – that existed at the time, and that he is fairly sure was 'not far from [the village of] Slitting Mill; and perhaps a mile back into the Chase'.

Dodd stated that he had parked his car, a *Ford Cortina*, on the grass-verge of the road that was adjacent to the pool and was munching on his lunch and reading a newspaper. 'It was a bloody stifling day – remember that summer, how hot it was? I remember swigging something to drink and having a bite when there was something moving right on the bank [of the pool].'

Dodd added that he was startled to see a creature that he estimated to be around six or seven feet long, slowly surface from the water; and that then proceeded to 'bask' on the banks of the pool. 'It sort of wriggled,' said Dodd, adding that 'it was like its whole body seemed to sort of shake or wobble as it moved'.

Dodd further explained that the animal had a serpent-like head and an 'oily' coloured skin. Its body was 'thick' and it seemed wholly unconcerned by his presence. 'I know it saw me – or saw the car, definitely – because it looked right in this direction and then just went back to what it was up to: just laying there.'

But what was most puzzling to the shocked Dodd was the fact that the animal seemed to have 'flippers near the front – or little feet'. He conceded that the animal may conceivably have had similar 'flippers' or 'feet' at its rear, but he explained that the 'back-end never came right out of the water; like as if it was trying to keep itself cool from being part [sic] in the water.'

Dodd watched astonished – and not a little concerned, unsurprisingly – for at least twenty minutes, after which time the animal simply slid softly back into the pond. He concluded: 'I wondered how a small pond like that might feed an animal that big for food [sic]. But what about its feet or the flippers: does that mean it might have been able to go from pool to pool for fish and things?' Highly intriguing questions, indeed they were; but they were also ones that neither of us could really answer to any meaningful degree.

Of course, having heard such accounts on several previous occasions meant that Paul Bell's story was not that unusual to me at all – even though it certainly involved what was without doubt an unknown animal of truly impressive proportions. But what elevated it to a far *stranger* level, was the fact that Bell claimed, quite matter-of-factly I have to confess, that the following Saturday he was fishing in practically the same spot, when 'I got the feeling I was being watched', and saw something equally monstrous – yet manifestly different.

Peering across the width of the canal, he was both horrified and petrified to see a dark, hairy face staring intently at him out of the thick, green bushes. The head of the animal was unmistakably human-like 'but crossed with a monkey' said Bell, who added that 'as soon as it saw me, up it went and ran right into the trees and I lost it'. He further explained: 'That was it; a second or two was all. But as it got up and ran, I knew it was a big monkey. But what flummoxed me more than seeing it though, was what was it doing there?' And that was a question I sincerely wanted answering, too.

To his credit, Bell did not elaborate or claim some dramatic long-lasting encounter; nor did he assert that he knew all of the dark secrets of the Man-Monkey, as Rob Lea had claimed back in the summer of 2000.

No: it was merely his wish to share with me the amazing facts of an astounding event that, for the most part, he had kept firmly hidden for what was, at the time of my interview with him, nearly a quarter of a century.

While making the ten-minute journey home from the *Old House at Home* on what was an appropriately dark and stormy night, I carefully considered time and again the fascinating story that Paul Bell had related to me. Yes, it was very similar indeed to many other tales of a distinctly Man-Monkey kind that had been related to me over the course of the previous few years; and so that, if nothing else, was a major plus in my book. But to find someone who claimed to have seen no less than *two* weird, cryptozoological entities in precisely the *same* location and both in the time-frame of just one week, seemed just *far* too good to be true.

But on the other hand, if Bell merely wanted to spin a tall yarn that he secretly thought I would likely buy, why on Earth would he introduce details of a *second* encounter that only had the inevitable knock-on effect of making the original tale seem far less than believable? Beyond filing the story for posterity, there was admittedly very little more that I could conceivably do with a twenty-something-year-old tale that had no additional witness testimony in support of it. I shook my head and continued on my way. Yet again, a story that linked the Man-Monkey with truly high-strangeness had crossed my path. But, once again, it seemed to provide me with more questions than answers.

And there was yet another story that reached my ears in this same, precise time-frame, that strongly suggested a mysterious – albeit poorly understood - link between sightings of wild-men-of-the-woods and water-based beasts. This one, brought to my attention by Eileen Gallagher, echoed that of Paul Bell almost to an almost uncanny degree.

Gallagher had telephoned me early one week-day morning, to relate how a friend of hers – named Janice - had undergone some sort of very traumatic encounter late at night with a man-beast in the village of Childs Ercall – which can be found in north Shropshire. Gallagher had lost touch with Janice in the late 1970s; however, she still well-recalled the salient facts. So the story went, it was back in 1971, and Janice was fifteen at the time and living in a nearby village. After an evening spent with her then-boyfriend at the home of his parents in Childs Ercall, Janice was happily riding her pedal-bike back home when she was shocked to see a large, hairy animal dash across the road directly in front of her, while simultaneously glaring at her in a menacing fashion as it did so. Eileen Gallagher recalled that Janice had told her that the animal was human-like in shape, was covered in long flowing dark hair, possessed a pair of bright yellow eyes that 'twinkled', and had a black-skinned and 'shiny' face.

Although Gallagher could recall nothing more of any real substance; she genially wished me well in my quest for the truth about the Man-Monkey. I have to say that this particular story completely fascinated me, for one specific reason: the Bigfoot-style entity seen by Janice in the Shropshire village of Childs Ercall was not the only weird creature said to inhabit this otherwise utterly normal and pleasant little English village. Indeed, legend has it that centuries ago a deadly mermaid was said to inhabit a pool there. In 1893, the writer Robert

Charles Hope described the story as follows:

'...there was a mermaid seen there once. It was a good while ago, before my time. I dare say it might be a hundred years ago. There were two men going to work early one morning, and they had got as far as the side of the pond in [a] field, and they saw something on the top of the water which scared them not a little. They thought it was going to take them straight off to the Old Lad himself! I can't say exactly what it was like, I wasn't there, you know; but it was a mermaid, the same as you read of in the papers. The fellows had almost run away at first, they were so frightened, but as soon as the mermaid had spoken to them, they thought no more of that. Her voice was so sweet and pleasant, that they fell in love with her there and then, both of them. Well, she told them there was a treasure hidden at the bottom of the pond - lumps of gold, and no one knows what. And she would give them as much as ever they liked if they would come to her in the water and take it out of her hands. So they went in, though it was almost up to their chins, and she dived into the water and brought up a lump of gold almost as big as a man s head. And the men were just going to take it, when one of them said: "Eh!" he said (and swore, you know), "if this isn't a bit of luck!" And, my word, if the mermaid didn't take it away from them again, and gave a scream, and dived down into the pond, and they saw no more of her, and got none of her gold. And nobody has ever seen her since then. No doubt the story once ran that the oath which scared the uncanny creature involved the mention of the Holy Name.'

Was it only a chance coincidence that both the Shropshire village of Childs Ercall, and Bridge 39 on the Shropshire Union Canal, were said to be equally haunted by hairy man-beasts, and bizarre water-based entities? This is a question that will be addressed in a later chapter; however, at *this* stage it is also worth noting that the county of Staffordshire – which borders upon Shropshire, and both of which have had far more than their fair share of Man-Monkey-type reports - is also home to a number of famous mermaid legends.

For example, the village of Thorncliffe, near Leek, Staffordshire, has a tale of a mermaid that can be seen at the `witching hour` at the appropriately named Mermaid's Pool. Those that get too close to the seemingly beautiful creature, as she combs her long and flowing locks under a moonlit sky, are destined to be dragged into the waters of the pool by what is in reality a malevolent, and utterly deadly, she-devil. Reputedly, the legend dates back to around the tenth century, when a young girl (who, so the story goes, may have been a witch who was well-practiced in the Black-Arts) was pursued and persecuted by a local man, who duly threw the girl to her death in the waters of Mermaid's Pool. She, in turn, screamed bloody vengeance upon her persecutor before she disappeared under the water and was duly drowned. And sure enough, the man's body was shortly thereafter found dead in Mermaid's Pool – his face violently torn to pieces, as if by monstrous talons. [1]

And then there is the mermaid of Aqualate Mere.

Situated barely a stone's throw from the Shropshire town of Newport and just over the border into Staffordshire, Aqualate Mere – at 1.5 kilometres long and 0.5 kilometres wide, it is the largest natural lake in the Midlands; yet is very shallow, extending down to little more than a uniform three feet. Hidden on a private estate by low-lying woodlands that are themselves dominated by alder and willow, fen meadow and wet pasture land, Aqualate Mere is home to a rich variety of wildlife, including the buzzard, the barn-owl, the mallard, the teal, the fox, the polecat, the otter, the mink, both pike and bream; and – notably - a thriving herd of Exmoor ponies. But it may be home to far stranger things, too.

Legend has it that one day many years ago, when the Mere was being cleaned, a mermaid ominously rose out of the water – scaring the life out of the work-men, not surprisingly – while simultaneously making dark threats to destroy the town of Newport if any attempt was ever made to empty Aqualate Mere. Very wisely, perhaps, the Mere was not drained. Notably, the Mere sits close to the A519 Road that runs right through the village of Woodseaves and close to Bridge 39, home of our old friend, the Man-Monkey.

---

1. For more details of this undeservedly obscure legend, we would suggest that you refer to Lisa Dowley's article in the 2007 CFZ Yearbook.

CHAPTER XI
THE HORN DANCE

The distinctly unusual, yet most definitely thought-provoking, Man-Monkey-related story of Mick Dodds, proved to be the very last one that I would personally investigate during the course of my enquiries; as some months later I moved to the United States to live. And, I suppose, somewhat appropriately, it also proved to be one of the most bizarre of all the many and varied cases that I delved into between 1986 and early 2001.

As I have extensively detailed, I had come across a veritable plethora of post-1879 Man-Monkey-style reports and encounters, that had occurred in the direct vicinity of Bridge 39 on the Shropshire Union Canal; and I had also uncovered the notable details of several, eerily similar incidents that had occurred deep within the confines of the nearby Cannock Chase woods of Staffordshire, and high atop the disaster-laden Tay Bridge in Scotland. But Mick Dodds' story, of distinctly dark goings-on that had their beginnings set firmly in the ancient Staffordshire village of Abbots Bromley, was quite unlike any other that I had ever come across - before and, I have to say, since even.

But before I delve into the heart of Dodds' remarkably odd account, a word - or several - first about Abbots Bromley: although certainly only a small village, it has become well-renowned for its famous 'Horn Dance' that is held every year on 'Wakes Monday', which follows the first Sunday - or 'Wakes Sunday' as it is known - after September 4. While the full and unexpurgated facts pertaining to the Dance have been somewhat obscured by the inevitable passage of time, the following can most certainly be said: the 'horns' that are themselves utilised in the dance are, in reality, reindeer antlers, that date back to at least 1065; and Wakes Monday aside, they can be found on constant display in the village's St. Nicholas Church.

At 8.00 a.m. on each and every Wakes Monday, twelve performers

comprised of :
(a)   six men whose job it is to hold the horns aloft throughout the dance;
(b)   a musician;
(c)   a young boy equipped with bow-and-arrow;
(d)   a 'Hobby Horse';
(e)   a woman playing the role of Maid Marion;
(f)   a traditional 'fool'; and
(g)   a boy with a triangle,

commence upon their magical parade through the streets of the village to a specific location where the dance duly kicks off in fine style. Music is supplied by a melodeon player; while the Hobby Horse beats a careful and rhythmic time with constantly snapping jaws. The high point of the dance occurs when the 'Deer-Men' face each other, and with horns duly lowered, act out a mock form of combat.

Much merriment and celebration inevitably follows, with the dancers and the ensuing throng making their ways to the various village inns and houses – and which continues well into the evening, and that is ultimately brought to a resounding close at around 8.00 p.m. with a Service of Compline (Church of England, final service of the day). In other words, a damned good time is truly had by one and all.

It must be said that while the Horn Dance is without a doubt the major event of the year for the village folk of Abbots Bromley, the precise origins of the centuries-old ceremony are still somewhat obscure. Some students of the Dance are firmly convinced that it was put into place to commemorate the assigning of hunting rights to the people of Abbots Bromley in centuries-long-past. Meanwhile, others see the Horn Dance as possibly being a relic celebration that honours the granting in 1226, by Henry II, of the three-day-long Berthelmy Fair. And then a third theory suggests even older origins for the Horn Dance: according to some, the Horn Dance may possibly be one of the very last surviving rituals that celebrate Britain's long-gone mysterious, and prehistoric, past. For example, the 'shooting' of the bow at the 'Deer-Men' is perceived in some quarters as being an act that has its origins fixed firmly within the world of ritual magic, when prehistoric man utilised both wild dance and ancient magic in a swirling and heady concoction designed to ensure a successful hunt for food.

But whatever the ultimate truth of the affair, even today, in the somewhat sterile and technology-driven years of the early twenty-first century, to personally attend Abbots Bromley's Horn Dance is to take an instant, curious and joyous journey into England's most mysterious past when myth, magic and folklore were all-dominating – as Mick Dodds found out all too graphically, and to his – and his wife's - personal psychological cost also.

According to Dodds, he had read the article on the Man-Monkey that Irene Bott and I had penned for the *Chase Post* back in the summer of 2000; but he had wavered for some months about whether or not he should contact us. Indeed, it would not be until early February 2001 that he finally did so. And while Dodds' alleged encounter did not occur at the site of a haunted bridge – as had so many of the other encounters with the Man-Monkey that I had personally investigated – it *did* contain that ever-present feature of so many such stories: namely that of a marauding, hairy man-beast that propelled itself in a truly violent fashion at the vehicle of the terrified witness late at night.

Dodds worked from nine-to five, Monday-to-Friday, in the historic city of Lichfield; and so we agreed on a meeting point at a café that was close to his work-place: namely, a small bric-a-brac shop situated only ten minutes walk from the city's old cathedral.

As we sat and drank cokes and ate beans on toast, Mick Dodds began his remarkable tale. It was in 1986 that he and his family had driven to attend – for the first time; and, as it would transpire, the *only* time – Abbots Bromley's Horn Dance. They stayed in the area all day, he told me, and duly rounded off the evening with hearty meals and refreshing drinks in a local public house. It was around 10.45 p.m. when Dodds, his wife, and mother-in-law left both the pub and the village of Abbots Bromley behind them: 'The bell had rung not long before; so I know the time roughly,' he explained to me.

And so, the trio duly began their journey home. Although the final destination of Dodds and his wife was Lichfield, a brief detour was required to take his mother-in-law back to her place of abode: which was a small house in the village of Stowe-by-Chartley. All was utterly normal until Dodds passed by the ancient and ruined Chartley

Castle that, today, overlooks the A518 road. Built on land that had come into the possession of the Earls of Chester as far back as the end of the 11th Century, Chartley Castle was a stone motte-and-bailey fortress founded in the thirteenth century by Ranulph Blundeville, the then Earl of Chester. Supported by the motte are, today, the still-standing remains of a rare cylindrical keep, with the inner bailey curtain wall still strongly flanked by two huge half-round towers, a gate-house, and an angle-tower. A strong counter-scarp bank and cross-ditch divides the inner and outer baileys, with another ditch and bank encasing the whole castle. Notably, Chartley Castle is to where – on Christmas Eve, 1585 – Mary, Queen of Scots was taken before being moved to Fotheringay for execution on February 8 of 1586.

And with that bit of background information out of the way, let us now return to the story of Mick Dodds. He would assert that after dropping his mother-in-law off at her home, he and his wife began the journey back to their own abode, and what they assumed would be a stress-free, night-time drive through Staffordshire's green and pleasant countryside. How completely and devastatingly wrong they were.

According to Dodds, as they drove along the road, and with Chartley Castle rapidly closing in, he was forced to violently and suddenly slam on the brakes as a huge stag ambled slowly – yet majestically, too – across the road directly in front of them. The sight of the massive beast was enough to both amaze and gob-smack Dodds and his wife in equal amounts; and the fact that they had come across the stag only mere hours after attending Abbots Bromley's Horn Dance, made for a very peculiar set of synchronistic circumstances indeed. But that was nothing at all compared to what supposedly happened next.

Dodds, realising how bizarre the next aspect of his story was surely going to sound to me, apologised profusely before he even began telling it! In return, I told him that no apology was necessary. Instead, I explained to him, I would much prefer to merely hear the facts and then try and firmly evaluate them for myself. And so, Mick Dodds duly began: as the huge stag made its slow yet deliberate way across the road, his wife suddenly screamed at the sight of what looked like a large chimpanzee that bounded after the stag from the darkness of the field that sat to the right of their car. Half way across the road, the 'chimpanzee' stopped suddenly, looked directly at the terrified husband and wife and, to their utter horror and consternation, charged their vehicle; but - at the last moment - backed away from actually causing any structural damage to the car, or physical harm to the fear-stricken pair.

Dodds said that in his overwhelming panic to quickly put the vehicle into reverse gear, he stalled its engine; and then - even worse still - ended up completely flooding it as he tried to re-start the car. As an inevitable result, the Dodds were briefly stranded in the road with a hairy monstrosity looming wildly in front of them. For about twenty seconds the beast stared at both husband and wife, and on two other occasions again headed for their vehicle at full speed, 'like it was going to attack', before finally bounding off to the left; and, so it appeared at least, in a direction that specifically followed that of the huge stag – which, by now, was seemingly long gone.

Dodds reiterated to me several times during the course of our conversation that he felt there was a most definite connection between the giant stag, the hairy man-beast, and the ancient, folklore-driven festival that he, his wife, and his mother-in-law, had attended only hours earlier at the old village of Abbots Bromley. But how and why, of course, he had no idea at all. And I didn't either - unfortunately. But Dodds *did* explain to me that it was my *C-Files* article on the fear-inducing actions of the Man-Monkey at Bridge 39 back in January 1879 that had prompted him to contact me. We discussed the case, and we went over the details, for nigh-on an hour, before I was completely certain that Dodds had related all of the relevant facts to me – as brief, as bizarre, and as tantalising as they most definitely were.

Was it possible, Dodds asked me, that he and his wife had possibly undergone some form of weird time displacement, in which our world had crossed paths with that of some type of prehistoric man, wildly chasing the stag – and all within the confines of an England long-gone and of a type which the Dodds family had been blessed (if that's the right word!) with only the very briefest of tantalising glimpses? Again, I had absolutely no answers. While Mick Dodds was somewhat visibly disappointed that I was unable to provide those answers to his encounter that he and his wife so yearned to uncover, after I carefully related to him the details of some of the other witness testimony that had come my way, he was at least pleased and relieved to learn that he and his wife were not mad, and were not the only people who had been plagued by late-night, nightmarish encounters with car-charging monkey-like entities in the English countryside.

There is a curious sequel to this distinctly odd affair.

My wife Dana and I spent most of 2006 living back in England. In the latter part of July of that year, I received a telephone call late one night from Wiltshire.

It was my good friend Matthew Williams – the only person in the world, thus far, who has been arrested, charged and duly convicted for making undercover of darkness a 'Pictogram'-style Crop Circle (in reality, the charge was causing damage to a field). Did I know, Matt asked me in somewhat excited tones, that a fairly complex Crop Circle design had appeared only days earlier next to Chartley Castle? No, I did not, I told him. But, after speaking with Matt, I was most certainly determined to go and see for myself what was afoot at Chartley Castle.

I had spent many a happy summer in the 1990s driving around the county of Wiltshire in search of Crop Circles – and on more than several occasions with Matt himself - but as this specific design was relatively close to the home of my father - who we were visiting at the time – Dana, my father and I drove up there to check out the evidence for ourselves. Sure enough, there was the huge Crop Circle, sitting in a field practically right next door to Chartley Castle. Not only that: lying strewn around the fringes of the Circle was a not inconsiderable pile of large and colourful peacock feathers.

So here I was, at a location that had been the site of a 1986 Man-Monkey style encounter, and that two decades later was home to nothing less than a giant Crop Circle and apparently at least one distinctly out-of-place peacock!

Again, I had no idea what – if indeed *anything* – all of this meant at a Fortean level; or even if it was all due to the effects of some giant, and complex, coincidence or synchronicity. Instead, I merely ensured that we secured a wealth of photographs of the Crop Circle, of Chartley Castle, and of the myriad peacock feathers. We scoured, searched and walked the area for an hour or so, and then headed on our way to a local inn for a well-earned pint of cider or several.

Back to 2001: For the rest of the next year and a half, things of a Man-Monkey nature were curiously and notably absent from my life. But, needless to say, that situation would eventually change.

CHAPTER XII
THE MAN-MONKEY RETURNS

In November 2002, quite out of the blue and while I was sat in my office, I received an email from the Midlands-based *Express & Star* newspaper asking if I could write an article for them on the nefarious exploits of none other than the Man-Monkey. The reasoning behind the request was a very simple one: only a couple of days earlier, Ray Wallace, an American, and one of the most controversial figures of all time in cryptozoology, passed away. For many years it had been said that Wallace had carried out numerous hoaxes in the Bigfoot arena – something that had led the sceptical community to vigorously, yet without any real justification, maintain that, had Wallace's dubious input not been in evidence, Bigfoot would simply not exist; period.

As cryptozoologist Loren Coleman noted after Wallace's death:

> 'Down through the years, Wallace would carry on pranks, be tied to carved fake Sasquatch feet, and produce and try to sell dubious photographs and films. He was a great letter writer and would pen long passages to magazine editors about this photograph or telling of how he knew a Bigfoot was nearby guarding a mine full of gold. After a while, most Bigfoot hunters and researchers took Wallace as merely a spinner of fanciful tall tales.'

In view of Wallace's passing, and coupled with the wholly unjustified claims of much of the world's media that without Wallace's involvement, there would be no Bigfoot at all, I duly wrote a feature for the *Express & Star* to the effect that while people were busily focusing all of their attentions upon Wallace, his many undoubted hoaxes, and on the possibility that America's most famous man-beast was nothing more than a tall-tale borne out of the infamous actions of the man himself, we would all do very well to wisely remember that the continental United States was not the only locale said to be home to such monstrous entities. And it was here that the Man-Monkey loomed into view again, as I detailed for the readers of the *Express & Star* the story of the dark and disturbing events at Woodseaves in January 1879. Then, in the wake of the publication of the article, something very weird began to happen.

All across the British Isles, reports of close encounters with spectral, hairy man-beasts of a distinctly Bigfoot-style nature began to surface. From deep within the confines of the mystical Sherwood Forest of Robin Hood infamy, to the leafy woods of northern England came all-manner of fantastic reports of everything hairy, glowing-eyed and monstrous.

But what, you may ask does this have to do with the Man-Monkey?

Okay, I'm getting there.

Shortly after the *Express & Star* published my article, I was contacted by Peter Rhodes, one of the senior feature-writers at the *Star* who had an interest in unusual phenomena such as unidentified flying objects and Bigfoot; but who also retained a healthy, yet fair-minded, scepticism about such issues, too. It transpired that in the immediate aftermath of the publication of the article, Rhodes had been contacted by a Staffordshire woman named Val Blackmore, whose son, Craig, had undergone a strange encounter while driving near the Cannock Chase one night in late 2002 – an encounter that eerily paralleled that of the Man-Monkey more than a century before. Peter Rhodes quickly wrote a follow-on article on this breaking and extraordinary event, but stressed to me in an email of January 6, 2003 that it 'may not see the light of day as young Craig seems reluctant to be photographed'. Fortunately, however, Rhodes' article *was* ultimately published in the *Star* on January 11, under the bold heading of *Night Terror with a British Bigfoot*.

Rhodes wrote: 'Whatever it was, it scared the living daylights out of Craig Blackmore. His mother Val says: "I have never seen Craig like that before. He came home shaking, absolutely petrified and white, as though he'd seen a ghost."'

According to Rhodes: 'Craig and a friend were convinced they had seen a huge, ape-like creature at the side of the road on Levedale

Lane between Stafford and Penkridge. Says Craig: "I was driving my [Ford] Fiesta [car] down the road towards Penkridge and as we approached a house, the security light came on. I saw something in the corner of my eye. It was coming towards the car, running very fast. It wasn't a dog or a deer. It was running like a human would run, but it was really hairy and dark. It came level and jumped at the car but just missed. My friend turned round and said it was huge and had run across the field. I turned the car around but there was no sign of it."'

The *Express & Star* article continued: 'The incident was over in seconds. A few minutes later, at the family home in Penkridge, mother and son tried to make sense of the bizarre experience. "I thought maybe Craig had been drinking, or perhaps someone had spiked a drink," says Val. "But that hadn't happened. He is a very truthful boy. He would not say something had happened if it hadn't. And anyway, his friend was in the same state of shock."'

Rhodes added: 'Although the event, eight weeks ago, had been terrifying, Craig, a 19-year-old HGV mechanic, did not report it to the police. He told a few friends ("they all laughed") and tried to forget the experience. And then, a few weeks later, the *Express & Star* carried a report by the Walsall UFO writer Nick Redfern on the legend of Bigfoot…And as Nick Redfern revealed, Britain has its own curious sightings. In January 1879 a man was riding home with his horse and cart to Ranton, near Stafford. About a mile from the village of Woodseaves, he was attacked by what he described as a creature "half-man and half-monkey."

'After the *Express & Star* carried Nick Redfern's account,' explained Rhodes, 'Craig's family got in touch with us to tell of his experience.' Rhodes contacted British Bigfoot researcher Geoff Lincoln for comment, who said: 'Bigfoot in Britain is an odd subject and very often the target of ridicule. But sightings are taking place and I am currently looking into two other reports in 2002, one in Northumberland and another in Lancashire.'

Peter Rhodes concluded his article thus: 'To Craig [Geoff Lincoln] offers a simple message worthy of *The X-Files*: "You are not alone."'

I had to admit to myself that this was without doubt a highly intriguing report: geographically speaking, the location of Craig Blackmore's experience was only a relatively short distance by car to Woodseaves. But most notable of all to me was the particular action of the strange man-beast. As in the encounter of January 1879, and as with that of Gavin in 1997, the events at Levedale Lane revolved around a hairy creature violently lashing out at someone who was making a late night trip home on a wood-shrouded road in central England. Indeed, the only real difference was that whereas, in 1879, the victim was with horse and cart, and was therefore afforded very little protection from the horrific assault, in the cases of both Craig Blackmore and Gavin, at least they had the safety of their cars to fall back on.

It must be said that the strange affair of Craig Blackmore was never really resolved; and yet I had to consider the strong possibility that, whatever the Man-Monkey was, it was most definitely active in the woods and forests of Staffordshire more than one hundred years after it had first burst forth out of the thick trees that enveloped the Shropshire Union Canal.

And 2002 was notable for a couple of additional reasons, too: first, it was also in that year that yet *another* report surfaced of an encounter with the Man-Monkey at the same wretched stretch of canal; one that had occurred back in the 1980s but that had remained hidden for years. The website waterscape.com described the story as follows:

'When British Waterways appealed for information about ghosts on the waterways in 2002, one respondent reported a more recent sighting of the ghost and thanked us for proving to his family that he was not seeing things! He told us that during a boating holiday on the "Shroppie" in the 1980s he took the tiller while the family were inside the boat preparing lunch. Passing under a bridge he looked up to see what he described as "a huge black, hairy monkey" staring down at him. Astonished, he called his family out to see the creature. But by the time the boat had passed under the bridge, the creature had vanished. The man said he had been teased by his wife and children ever since over his sighting of the phantom monkey and was grateful to hear that others had seen it, too.'

Then there was the encounter of Mike Atkins – an encounter that had taken place back in 1996; but that Atkins had steadfastly decided to keep firmly to himself until he read my *Express & Star* article in December 2002 on the exploits of the Man-Monkey. Not only that: Atkins' story eerily paralleled that of both Craig Blackmore in 2002 and the man at Woodseaves in 1879. Atkins' encounter had not occurred at Woodseaves or on the Cannock Chase, however, but at the Blithfield Reservoir, Staffordshire. According to Atkins, he was driving over the road-bridge that crosses the reservoir in the early hours of a particular morning in 1996 when a giant, hairy animal 'practically launched itself across the road at my car'. Fortunately, Atkins was able to floor the accelerator, and thus both nimbly and skilfully avoided having to engage the wild animal in near hand-to-hand combat, as did the unfortunate victim at Bridge 39 back in 1879. There was nothing more that Atkins wished to impart (although I *did* detect from his concise words that there was much more that he probably *could* have imparted); and so, after a brief yet cordial telephone conversation one evening in late December 2002, I quickly transferred my hastily scribbled pencil notes into a Microsoft Word document on my computer, happily content in the fact that apparent encounters with beasts that sounded suspiciously like the Man-Monkey were still continuing to trickle in.

And, now, with the currently-available data and the witness testimony both firmly in-hand and digested, we have to ask ourselves: what *was* the true nature of the beast seen on that fateful night back in 1879 – and, indeed, ever since? Was it an ape of some type, possibly even one that had escaped from the confines of a private zoo? Was it a wholly paranormal entity that had its origins in some dark and far-off twilight realm? Or could it have been something else entirely? Throughout the period of my own, personal studies of the Man-Monkey – from 1986 to early 2001 – these were the very questions that had always plagued me. And so, with the above in mind, I will now provide you with the answers and theories that came my way during that heady period.

CHAPTER XIII
WHO GOES THERE?

Let us begin with the theory – as far-fetched as it almost certainly may be – that a real-life, flesh-and-blood animal of distinctly exotic origins was wildly on the loose, roaming the dark woods near Woodseaves back in 1879. Impossible, you say.

Well…yes…probably.

I say *probably* rather than *definitely*, though, because of the very strange and surreal story of Dr. John Kerr Butter.

More than a century ago, the good doctor was both a resident of the town of Cannock, Staffordshire and a keen and renowned zoologist. Indeed, it is a little-known – and truly startling – fact that Butter possessed a highly impressive collection of exotic animals that were housed at his place of residence on the town's Wolverhampton Road, and which astonishingly enough included giraffes, monkeys, elephants, ostriches, emus, geese, kangaroos, and a peculiar Madagascan cat-like creature called a fossa that is related to the mongoose. Butter had even tamed a wild ocelot that he kept on his property; a certainly considerable feat that justifiably earned him the distinction of being made a Fellow of the Royal Zoological Society.

Somewhat amusingly, Butter would regularly make house-calls to his patients sat atop a trap that would be wildly pulled around the town of Cannock by a fully-grown zebra! And for those patients that were able to make it to his surgery, they would invariably be greeted by `Antony`, the doctor's favourite, tiny pet monkey. Interestingly, Butter was also a recognised expert on big cats and he provided regular animal welfare for the varied traveling menageries that visited the town of Cannock, as well as the surrounding towns and villages. In addition, Dr. Butter was a devoted collector of strange artifacts, which included bear-skins, an ink-stand constructed from the jaw of an alligator, and countless jars full of preserved animal organs. But there is still more to come: much more, in fact.

On one occasion Dr. Butter went to do battle: namely, at the turn of the twentieth century in the Boer War. And it is a known and verifiable fact that at least *some* of his animals *did* disappear from his property during this particular period when he was far away from home. Moreover, at the outbreak of the First World War in 1914, *all* of Dr. Butter's animals promptly vanished – as a direct result of the nation's dwindling food supplies, something which ensured an unfortunate lack of adequate sustenance for Butter's ever-over-flowing menagerie. Notably, there is *no record whatsoever* of what happened to the doctor's huge and varied collection of exotic beasts in this crucial period of British zoological (and perhaps even cryptozoological) history.

Is it possible that Dr. Butter – who was an undoubted, life-long animal lover – secretly released his beloved beasts back into the wild, perhaps on a dark night, when the prying eyes of the town-folk of Cannock would no longer be upon him? Needless to say, of course, if a fully-grown elephant or a zebra were roaming the wilder parts of Staffordshire in the early part of the twentieth century, we surely would have heard about it long ago. Therefore, it seems safe to assume that these creatures, at least, found new homes in local zoos or perhaps in travelling circuses.

But, it is an undeniable fact that the Cannock Chase *has* for decades been the reported home of large, exotic cats, and kangaroos (or possibly wallabies) - animals that most assuredly *were* housed at the doctor's property on Cannock's Wolverhampton Road. The possibility that at least *some* of today's creatures roaming the area might very well be the direct descendents of those same animals lovingly kept and cared for by Dr. Butter – who may very well have wished them their freedom, rather than risk having them destroyed – *must* rank highly, even if some prefer to dismiss such admittedly fantastic and controversial ideas.

And what was the fate of Antony, the doctor's beloved little monkey? Certainly, no-one knows. If tiny Antony was also released into the wilds of Staffordshire, is it possible that Butter had released *other*, somewhat similar creatures – chimpanzees, perhaps – into some of the dark woods and forests of the area in earlier times, say around, oh, January 1879, and near a certain bridge on the Shrop-shire Union Canal? And, if so, is it remotely possible that they have been secretly breeding and living in stealth ever since?

Admittedly, this is a purely hypothetical scenario (and, some might say, a wholly outlandish and over-the-top scenario, too), and there is certainly no hard data *at all* to prove or disprove *anything* of sub-stance on this particular issue – beyond the undeniable fact that from the latter part of the 1800s to the early years of the 20th Century, dis-tinctly exotic animals from all across the world were kept at a loca-tion not at all far from the infamous Bridge 39 near Woodseaves. If Dr. John Kerr Butter *was* in any way implicated in the strange affair of the Man-Monkey, then he certainly took his strange secrets to the grave with him when he died – in his mid-sixties – in 1920.

And lest anyone think that this is the only example of physically real, exotic beasts having been housed in the Midlands in years and cen-turies past, consider both carefully and thoughtfully the following:

Only a handful of miles from the fringes of the Cannock Chase, and specifically near the town of Brewood, stands Chillington Hall, where, in the 1500s, one of the first private zoos was established – by nobleman Sir John Gifford. According to legend, on one fateful day, Sir John's favourite animal, a leopard no less, broke out of the con-fines of its enclosure and escaped into the wilds of the surrounding Staffordshire countryside. Arming himself with a cross-bow, Sir John, along with his son, quickly set off in hot pursuit of the maraud-ing animal and, to his horror found it poised to attack a terror-stricken mother and child.

In an instant, according to the story at least, Sir John quickly drew his bow and took careful aim. At that instant, his son cried out: 'Prenez haliene, tirez fort,' or: 'Breathe deep, pull hard.' Sir John sen-sibly, and quickly, took his son's advice and fired. With but one shot, the leopard fell to the floor, utterly dead. Gifford's cross – which still stands to this day – was raised where the creature supposedly took its final, gasping breath, and Sir John duly adopted his son's words as the family's motto.

If one large, exotic cat was roaming the wilds of Staffordshire as far back as the 1500s, then who can say how many other escapees there may have been that *weren't* cut down by Sir John's masterful skills with the bow and arrow? It is a sobering thought indeed to think that large, wild cats were possibly living stealthily in the woods of Staffordshire more than five hundred years ago.

Of course, there is a world of difference between a large, monkey-like animal and an exotic big cat. However, where one truly out-of-place beast lurks, perhaps another one may be found, too.

CHAPTER XIV
THE HAIRY HANDS
AND OTHER THINGS

Even if the unearthly saga of the Man-Monkey cannot be readily explained in terms of a purely physical animal or animals, there are still several other viable options available to us. They are options, however, that take us down some very dark roads indeed; and specifically into those strange areas and realms that relate to the worlds of both the paranormal and the occult.

The Man-Monkey of the Shropshire Union Canal aside, a study of British folklore, history and mythology reveals a veritable host of additional tales pertaining to historic encounters with spectral, monkey-like animals. The Ghost-Ape of Marwood, for example, was, when alive, said to be a pet of a local land-owner who one day grabbed the land-owner's young son and climbed into a tree with him, refusing to come down – something that quickly resulted in the animal being killed. However, and somewhat intriguingly, after the death of the beast, its spectral form was said to roam the woods of the surrounding area late at night.

Then there is the centuries-old tale of Martyn's Ape, a ghostly creature rumoured to haunt Athelhampton House in Dorset – and which was supposedly the pet of a member of the Martyn family that was either:

(a) Accidentally bricked up alive during construction work;
(b) Entombed along with a family-member, who committed suicide in a locked, secret room, or:
(c) Walled-up by an unforgiving parent.

The Martyn family had built the earliest part of the house in the fifteenth century; and, notably, the family motto was: 'He who looks at Martyn's ape, Martyn's ape will look at him.' Oddly, although the story of Martyn's Ape is a well-known one, not a single named witness to the beast's alleged activities has, thus far at least, ever been identified.

And from darkest Devonshire comes a strange tale of something eerily similar: namely the macabre story of the Hairy-Hands. It was around 1910 that the weird saga supposedly began – on what is today the B3212 road, in the vicinity of the Dartmoor locales of Postbridge and Two Bridges. Somewhat disturbingly, and as with the cases at Bridge 39, and those incidents involving Gavin, Craig Blackmore, and Mike Atkins, something hairy and unknown would time and again violently lash out at unwary passing drivers, and which, in one case, reportedly even resulted in a tragic death for one unfortunate road-user.

In most cases, victims of the diabolical phenomenon reported large, hairy and 'disembodied hands' firmly grabbing the steering wheel of their vehicle – or the handle-bars of their bike - unsurprisingly striking complete terror into their hearts, and which invariably resulted in them being violently forced off the country road. For a decade or so, the events were considered nothing more than a mild – albeit certainly sinister - curiosity for the superstitious locals of Dartmoor. However, that situation would drastically change in 1921.

In June of that year, Dr. E.H. Helby, who was at the time serving as the Medical Officer at the nearby Dartmoor Prison, was tragically killed when he lost control of his motor-cycle and sidecar, in the latter of which were seated his two children. Helby had just about enough time to warn his children to jump to safety – which they did – before he was thrown from his motorcycle and instantly killed.

Then, on the dull, foggy day of August 26 of the same year, a young British Army captain – described as being 'a very experienced rider' – was also thrown into the verge of the road, after he too lost control of his motor-cycle. The captain stated at the time: 'It was not my fault. Believe it or not, something drove me off the road. A pair of hairy hands closed over mine. I felt them as plainly as ever I felt anything in my life – large, muscular, hairy hands. I fought them for all I was worth, but they were too strong for me. They forced the machine into the turf at the edge of the road, and I knew no more till I came to myself, lying a few feet away on my face on the turf.'

And there was much more to come.

In the summer of 1924, the well-known and widely-respected Devonshire folklorist Theo Brown was camping in a caravan, approximately half a mile from the road in question; and, in later life, would detail a particularly nightmarish, and nighttime, encounter that occurred years before.

Brown wrote:

> 'I knew there was some power very seriously menacing us near, and I must act very swiftly. As I looked up to the little window at the end of the caravan, I saw something moving, and as I stared, I saw it was the fingers and palm of a very large hand with many hairs on the joints and back of it, clawing up and up to the top of the window, which was a little open. I knew it wished to do harm to my husband sleeping below. I knew that the owner of the hand hated us and wished harm, and I knew it was no ordinary hand, and that no blow or shot would have any power over it. Almost unconsciously I made the Sign of the Cross and I prayed very much that we might be kept safe. At once the hand slowly sank down out of sight and I knew the danger was gone. I did say a thankful prayer and fell at once into a peaceful sleep. We stayed in that spot for several weeks but I never felt the evil influence again near the caravan. But, I did not feel happy in some places not far off [sic] and would not for anything have walked alone on the moor at night or on the Tor above our caravan.'

Then there was the story told to the writer Michael Williams (author of *Supernatural Dartmoor*) by journalist Rufus Endle, who maintained that while driving near Postbridge on an undetermined date, 'a pair of hands gripped the driving wheel and I had to fight for control'. Luckily, he managed to avoid crashing the vehicle; the hands simply vanished into thin air. A concerned Endle requested that the story specifically not be published until after his death.

And what are we to make of the spectral ape of Dundonald Castle, Scotland? Situated atop a large hill that overlooks northern Kilmarnock, the castle's origins can be traced back to the twelfth century, when one Walter, the High Steward of King David I, constructed a wooden fort high on the hill. Then, a century later, a far more formidable and sturdy structure was built, and Dundonald Castle steadily began to take shape. However, during the Wars of Independence with England in the fourteenth century, much of the castle was decimated and well and truly raised to the ground. It was, however, rebuilt according to the wishes of King Robert II and still remains standing centuries later. But that is not all...

According to Scottish researcher Mark Fraser, a remarkable and terrifying encounter with a spectral ape took place near the castle in 1994: 'Josephine Aldridge...says she will never go up the hill again as long as she lives...While walking on the hill her two Labradors suddenly went berserk, running around in circles...Then Josephine saw "this huge creature" that appeared some distance to the side of her...It did not seem to be solid, as Josephine could see the grass of the hill through its body, but it was covered in "longish, charcoal-coloured hair."'

Fraser added: '...it was nor dissimilar to a gorilla in shape, although it stood well over ten feet tall on two legs. When confronted by the strange sight Josephine began to pray; the creature after a few moments slowly faded out of sight...'

Mark Fraser was also told of the 1994 encounter at Torphins, near the Scottish city of Aberdeen. Fraser stated that: '...Pete and George... were driving along the road into Torphins, approximately two miles from their first meeting. In the witnesses' own words: "Suddenly from the side of the road there came this great muscular, hairy figure bounding out, which started to run behind the car. At one point it caught up and ran alongside the vehicle..."' Fraser added that: "Pete describes the creature as 'strong and muscular...red, glowing eyes... body covered in hair...about six feet five inches...jet black."'

Following the publication of the 2002 Man-Monkey-like encounter of Craig Blackmore, none other then BBC Television personality, weatherman, and star of *The Morning Show*, Ian McCaskill became embroiled in the mystery of the Cannock Chase Bigfoot when he headed to the area in hot pursuit of the mysterious creature. The BBC was full of good-humour as it reported on McCaskill's adventures on the Chase: 'Apparently he's hairy, giant and ape-like. And not at all the sort of person you want to bump into in a deserted place, on a dark night. Unfortunately, "Bigfoot", or the "Yeti" as it's become known, is out and about, on the prowl, and could be coming to a place near you.'

The BBC continued: 'Never fear, for the *Morning Show's* gallant Ian McCaskill was here. In the first week of February, he went off to Cannock Chase in Staffordshire to hunt down the eight-foot Yeti spotted recently in the area. A UK website devoted to Bigfoot research contains many reports, including yet another Staffordshire sighting. Lots of sightings occur near telecom towers, and one of the theories is that apparitions are caused by radiation surges from these towers.' But far stranger things were afoot. Indeed, in January 2003 an expedition to the wooded Bolam Lake in the north of England was undertaken by the Centre for Fortean Zoology, following bizarre sightings of a hairy, Bigfoot-like animal that were then being reported with unsettling regularity. As the CFZ recorded after the quest was completed:

> In the latter part of 2002 and early 2003, there occurred a huge 'flap' of Big Hairy Men (BHM) sightings throughout the British Isles that we could not afford to ignore and that required our immediate attention. Indeed, such was the scale of this extraordinary wave of encounters that, even as we made firm plans for an expedition in March, a handful of new sightings of large, man-beasts from the Bolam Lake area of Northumberland, England, arrived in our e-mail In-Box in January that prompted us to undertake an immediate study of the evidence.

> We liaised very closely with Geoff Lincoln, an absolutely invaluable researcher based in the area. We gave him our planned arrival time, and asked if any of the eye-witnesses would be prepared to speak to us. Much to our ever-lasting delight, five out of the six were. We think it should be noted here that the sixth is a soldier; and with the burgeoning situation in the Middle East spiraling rapidly out of control, it would be completely unreasonable to expect a serving military man to be at the beck-and-call of the CFZ.

> Serendipitously, we were able to stay at a house owned by our County Durham representative, David Curtis. He and his wife, Joanne, were absolutely fantastic all the way through our sojourn in the North. The only sad thing about our stay with them was that Davy had to work most of the time, and so, therefore, was not able to join us during most of our activities.

> After a series of fairly dull misadventures, we met Geoff Lincoln and Dr. Gail Nina-Anderson (a

member of the CFZ Board of Consultants), and we made our way in convoy to Bolam Lake itself. It would be nice to be able to say that we were overwhelmed with a spooky feeling, or that the *genus-loci* of the location were in some way redolent of Fortean freakiness. But it wasn't at all. It was just what one would expect from a heavily wooded country-park in the North of England in the middle of January - cold, wet and grey.

Geoff showed us three of the locations where these things had been reported. We carried out a thorough series of photographic mapping exercises, and did our best to fend off the incessant inquiries from the press. Just after lunchtime, a TV crew from a local television company arrived and filmed interviews with our investigation team. It was only after they had gone that we realised something very strange was happening.

Although we had tested all of our electronic equipment the night before, had charged up batteries where necessary, and had even put new batteries in all of our equipment that needed them, practically without exception all of our new equipment failed. The laptop, for example, has a battery, which usually lasts between 20 and 35 minutes. It lasted just three minutes before failing.

Admittedly, we received an enormous number of telephone calls during our stay at the lake, but not anywhere near enough to justify the fact that we had to change handsets four times in as many hours. The batteries in both Geoff's and our tape-recorders also failed. It seems certain that there was some strange electromagnetic phenomenon at work here.

Later that afternoon, we drove to a local pub where we met our first witnesses. Like all of the other people we were to meet over the next few days, they requested anonymity, and therefore in accordance with our strict confidentiality policy, we have respected this. Naomi and her son had been visiting Bolam Lake only a few days before. Not believing any of the reports that had appeared in the local media, they were both appalled and frightened when - while walking across the car-park itself - they had seen a huge creature standing motionless in the woods. They described an intense feeling of fear and trepidation, and rapidly left the area. They were incredibly co-operative, and agreed to come back to the lake with us the next day to stage a reconstruction.

We had a wake-up call at 5.30 a.m. the next morning, followed by a taxi-ride to a rest area five-hundred yards along the road from the Bolam Lake car-park, where we did a two-and-a-half minute interview for the BBC Radio 4 *Today* programme. One thing of great importance happened during the half-hour or so spent shivering by the side of the road waiting to speak to the BBC. Just before dawn, the crows, which live in a huge colony in the woods, started an appalling noise. Suddenly, the noise stopped; but was then followed by a brief succession of booming noises – like a heavily-amplified heartbeat from a Pink Floyd record – before the crows started up again. It is unclear whether these noises came from the vicinity of the lake itself or were made by the set-up of satellite dishes, and recording equipment that was loaded in the back of, and on top of, the BBC man's car. During the taxi journey back to Seaham, the driver remarked on the peculiar behaviour of the crows, and said that although he was a country-man himself and had spent his whole life living in this area, he had never heard anything quite like it.

On arriving back at base, it was time for the entire CFZ expeditionary force to drive to the outskirts of the city of Newcastle where we met Geoff and a second witness in a café attached to a garden center. The witness, Neil, had been fishing at Bolam Lake one night four or five years previously. Together with two companions he had been making his way back to the car-park when they encountered a huge, dark, man-shaped object about 7-8 ft in height with what he described as sparkling eyes. The three fishermen did not stop to investigate but ran back to the car.

However, this was by no means the only encounter that Neil had reported to us. Together with one of his companions from the first adventure, he had again been night fishing at Bolam Lake during the summer of 2002. They had been camped out on this occasion, and had heard noises, which they assumed were from an enormous animal moving around in the bushes outside of their camp. Deciding that discretion was most definitely the better part of valour, they decided not to investigate any further; but when they broke camp the next morning they found that the fish they had stored in a bait-tin had been taken, and there were distinct signs that something very large had been lumbering around in the immediate vicinity.

Possibly the most astounding story that he had to recount had taken place a couple of summers before our visit. He had been in the woods at the opposite side of the lake with his girl-friend. They had been making love, when his girlfriend told him she that she could see what she thought was a man in a monkey suit watching their sexual adventures from behind a bush.

Neil, unsurprisingly, looked around the area but could find nothing.

We then continued to the lake. Neil had been amazingly co-operative, and had, like Naomi, agreed to stage a reconstruction with us. At the lake we liaised with the team from a local investigative group called Twilight Worlds and began a series of exercises, which would take up the rest of the day. Geoff had noted, the previous week, a series of apparently artificial tree formations similar to those "Bigfoot Teepees" noted by researchers in the United States.

Together with Twilight Worlds, Geoff and CFZ stalwart Graham Inglis, went off to map these formations and to make a photographic record. They also took with them a Twilight Worlds member trained in using their EMF meter, together with a dowser. After our electrical mishaps of the previous day, we wanted to find out whether there were, indeed, any abnormal EMF fields in the area. Neither investigator found any unusual readings.

Our next task was to stage a reconstruction of Naomi's sighting. Again a full photographic and video record was made, and EMF readings were also taken. Again no unusual readings were recorded either by the EMF meter or the dowser. We then repeated the exercise with Neil and reconstructed his first sighting.

At about half-past-four, one of the members of Twilight Worlds reported seeing something large, human-shaped and amorphous in the woods directly in front of the car-park. As the dusk gathered at about 5 o'clock, we again heard the raucous noise of the crows that he had reported just before dawn. Suddenly, once again, they fell silent and one of the Twilight Worlds members shouted that she could hear something large moving around among the undergrowth. All of the car-drivers present were ordered to switch on their headlights and to put them on full-beam. We did not hear any noise in the undergrowth; although other people present did. Eight people were watching the woods and five of us saw an enormous man-shaped object run from right to left, disappear, and then a few moments later run back again.

When the expedition returned on Monday, we conducted experiments to find out exactly how far away the creature – if it was a creature – was from the excited onlookers. We were able to make a fairly accurate estimate that the creature had been one-hundred-and-thirty-four-feet away at the time of our sighting. We also estimated that the creature had run along a distance of between twelve and eighteen feet.

About five minutes after the encounter, we wandered across the car-park to the location when Naomi had reported seeing the creature. There, too, a sensation was felt of intense fear.

After an incident like that, anything else would have been an anti-climax. However, Geoff Lincoln took the CFZ team to interview two further witnesses. The first was a young man living in the suburbs of Newcastle, who told us of his encounter with an enormous man-shaped being next to a hollow tree in the woods, some months previously. The incident had taken place while he had been walking his dog. He had been so frightened by his experience that he refused to ever go near the lake again. Finally, we went to another pub where we met another man called Neil. He had been with the first Neil at the time of his initial sighting.

We were all impressed by his sincerity and by the way that he corroborated his friends' testimony in what seemed to us, at least, to be a very natural and wholly uncontrived manner. One day later, we all returned to the lake. We proceeded to carry out a thorough photographic survey of the final two sighting locations to ascertain – as far as was possible, at least – the size of the thing that had been seen on Saturday night, and its approximate distance from the eye-witnesses.

As the EMF scans had been remarkably unsuccessful, we tried to scan the area for magnetic anomalies using a pocket compass. Mike Hallowell, a friend and excellent researcher, registered a strange magnetic anomaly at the location of the fisherman's first sighting. However, it must be reported that when the team tried to replicate this later in the day, they were unsuccessful.

That evening, we interviewed a final witness: a woman in her late fifties who had been visiting the lake about five years before with her son who was then eleven years old. Like Naomi, she reported intense feelings of not exactly hostility; but what she interpreted as a message not to investigate a peculiar tree formation any further. She discussed these tree formations with us at some length. She had been surprised to find them at several locations throughout the woodlands. Our work was then finished and we returned home.

It quickly becomes apparent upon reading the above report that it contains several key ingredients that are also integral to the saga of the Man-Monkey. First, there was the reaction of the local bird population at Bolam, which very closely paralleled the ingredients of the story of Simon and his summer 1982 encounter at Woodseaves. Then there was the apparent effect that the presence of the Bolam Beast had on the team's electrical equipment – which was strikingly similar to Bob Carroll's experience – and his car trouble - at Bridge 39 in the early 1970s.

And then there was the actual nature of the beast itself: it was quite clearly not a real, physical animal – at least, not in a way that the term generally implies. Rather, it was as if the beast was 'one-dimensional' in nature. And if that were not enough, there was the manner of the creature's memorable disappearance. It did not vanish into the safety of the surrounding undergrowth or the trees. No, it *literally* vanished: just as had the Man-Monkey back on that fateful January 1879 night, in fact.

CHAPTER XV
ON THE TRAIL
OF THE KELPIE

If the Man-Monkey was not a purely physical animal in the sense that we strictly understand the term, but was perhaps far more spectral in nature – as *some* of the facts, at least, seem to strongly suggest – then how do we even begin to try and explain and reconcile this? There is one particular avenue that is most definitely worth exploring, and it is an avenue that has its origins buried deep within the history of ancient Scottish folklore. The Man-Monkey may be what is surely that most dastardly of all creatures: a Kelpie.

According to Scottish legend, the Kelpie – or the water-horse – is a wholly supernatural creature that haunts the rivers and the lochs of ancient Scotland and that has the uncanny ability to shape-shift. The most common form that the Kelpie takes is that of a horse – hence the name. It stands by the water's edge, tempting any passing and weary traveller that might consider continuing on his or her journey to mount it.

That, however, is always the fatal downfall of the traveller, as invariably the beast is then said to rear violently and charge head-long into the depths of the river or loch, and thus drowning its terrified rider in the process. Very notably, the Kelpie was also said to be able to transform itself into both a beautiful maiden, or *mermaid*, and a *large, hairy man* that would hide in the vegetation of Scottish waterways and *leap out and attack* the unwary [Italics all mine]. It must be noted too that the description of a 'large, hairy man' could equally apply to that most definitive of all shape-shifter's – namely the werewolf – seen at Bridge 39 in 1982 by Simon and a friend, and graphically described in other encounters in the area by the somewhat mysterious and enigmatic Rob Lea.

Of course, the Kelpie may simply be a denizen of the world of folklore and nothing else at all. But the parallels between the Scottish legends and the events at Bridge 39 in 1879 are truly – and undeniably - remarkable. The Kelpie could appear as a hair-covered hominid that would lurk within the lush greenery of Scotland's waters – just like the Man-Monkey. The Kelpie would reportedly violently attack passers-by – as did both the Man-Monkey and the creature seen near the waters of Blithfield Reservoir by Mike Atkins in 1996. And, of course, there is the fact that the Kelpie was said to be a much-feared killer of human beings; as the Man-Monkey may well have been, too.

And on this very important, latter point: you will recall that the police in the vicinity of Bridge 39 had *specifically* associated the sightings of the strange creature at Woodseaves in 1879 with the then recent death of a man who had unfortunately 'drowned in the cut'. The several parallels with the world of the Kelpie are, without doubt, truly uncanny. It goes without saying that none of this proves that Kelpies exist, of course – either in the world of the normal or even indeed in the world of the paranormal. It does, however, strongly suggest a belief in, and an acceptance of, Kelpie-like entities in rural Shropshire and Staffordshire by elements of the British Police Force, no less, in the latter part of the 19th Century – which is without doubt extraordinary.

It also suggests that if the latter day Man-Monkey reports are genuine (and I personally see no reason to dispute them or their attendant sources), then far from being merely a harmless relic of centuries-old Scottish folklore, the Kelpie is still among us, still thriving, and still up to its infernal activities. And one other thought while we are discussing all-things of a Kelpie-like nature: could it be that the large eel-like beast seen by fisherman Paul Bell in the hot summer of 1976 was in reality a Kelpie-style shape-shifter that, one week after his initial encounter, assumed for the *same* startled witness the form of the diabolical Man-Monkey? Ancient Scottish legend and folklore would certainly seem to suggest so. And, if that was the case, Bell can most definitely count his lucky stars that he did not pay for the encounter with both his soul and his life.

We should also note that the Shropshire village of Childs Ercall has legends of hairy wild-men and mermaids attached to it; and Aqualate Mere – *very* close to Woodseaves; the home of the Man-Monkey, no less – is also reputedly the lair of a beautiful mermaid. It must be said that sightings of beautiful mermaids and maidens, as well as hairy monstrosities, are the veritable hallmark of the presence of a shape-shifting Kelpie; as well as being two of its most preferred forms of appearance after that of the traditional water-horse.

It is also important to note that several other stretches of canal and certain waterways within the British Isles have curious folk-tales attached to them that are inextricably linked with both monkeys and bridges. For example, the village of Defford, Worcestershire, is home to a pub called the *Cider House*. One of the very few still-existing traditional cider houses in England, it has been in the same family for a century and a half, and visitors to the *Cider House* will find their drinks served to them in quaint pottery mugs, and amid a welcome atmosphere that harks back to a time long gone. More notable is the fact that for the locals that frequent the *Cider House*, it has a distinctly different moniker: namely, the *Monkey House*. So the legend goes, many years ago, a regular customer charged breathlessly into the pub late one night, claiming to have fallen into dense bramble bushes, after being attacked by…*a group of monkeys*. Notably, the village of Defford is situated close to Eckington, whose historic Eckington Bridge spans the River Avon.

Then there is the intriguingly named Monkey Marsh Lock. Situated on the Kennet and Avon Canal, it weaves its way through the Thames and the River Avon, and links the city of London with the British Channel. It is scheduled to be designated as an ancient monument and it is one of the only-two-remaining turf-sided locks in England of the type that were chiefly used in the early 1700s. Needless to say, the origins of the lock's admittedly eye-opening name remain shrouded in mystery.

And what of the so-called Monkey Island-Isleworth Canal Project of 1793? An ambitious plan first proposed in 1770 (but ultimately never brought to successful fruition) it was designed to link Maidenhead and Isleworth via a planned stretch of canal that would by-pass the River Thames. Monkey Island is a story in itself. The island is a small piece of land on the Thames that can be found near to the Berkshire village of Bray. Its name is actually derived from the Old English term: *Monks Eyot* – meaning Monks' Island, and was specifically named after a group of monks that resided at Amerden Bank, which is situated near to Bray Lock on the Buckinghamshire banks of the river.

In the early 1720s, the island came into the possession of the third Duke of Marlborough, Charles Spencer, and who duly oversaw the construction of a fishing lodge and temple. Monkey Island Lodge (which today still stands – but as a pavilion) was built completely out of wood. Notably, the artist Andieu de Clermont was asked to provide the Lodge with his own unique brand of paintwork – and he most certainly did so: 'grotesque gentleman monkeys', engaged in scenes of fishing, boating and shooting adorned a small room in the Lodge, and can still be seen there to this day.

In 1738, Lady Hertford described Monkey Island Lodge thus: '[It] has a small house upon it, whose outside represents a farm – the inside what you please: for the parlour, which is the only room in it except the kitchen, is painted upon the ceiling in grotesque, with monkeys fishing, shooting, etc., and its sides are hung with paper. When a person sits in this room he cannot see the water though the island is not above a stone's cast over; nor is he prevented from this by shade; for, except for six or eight walnut trees and a few orange trees in tubs there is not a leaf upon the island; it arises entirely from the river running very much below its banks.'

Roughly a century later, the Lodge had become a river-side inn, accessible only by ferry; that is until 1956, when a foot-bridge was finally built. And although the island's curious name seems to have wholly down-to-earth origins, it is intriguing to note that, once again, here is yet a locale in the British Isles linked with canals, bridges and 'grotesque monkeys'.

CHAPTER XVI
BLACK DOG PARALLELS

There is yet another angle that needs to be firmly addressed as part of our effort to try and determine what the Man-Monkey was, or indeed what it was not; and it is a theory that is inextricably linked with the tales of the ghostly, black devil dogs of old England. But before we address the several links between these two diabolical phenomena, some necessary background data on these rumoured hounds of hell is required.

In his definitive book on the subject *Explore Phantom Black Dogs*, author and researcher Bob Trubshaw wrote thus:

> 'The folklore of phantom black dogs is known throughout the British Isles. From the Black Shuck of East Anglia to the Mauthe Dhoog of the Isle of Man there are tales of huge spectral hounds "darker than the night sky" with eyes "glowing red as burning coals". The phantom black dog of British and Irish folklore, which often forewarns of death, is part of a worldwide belief that dogs are sensitive to spirits and the approach of death, and keep watch over the dead and dying. North European and Scandinavian myths dating back to the Iron Age depict dogs as corpse eaters and the guardians of the roads to hell. Medieval folklore includes a variety of "Devil dogs" and spectral hounds.'

Interestingly, one area that seems to attract more than its fair share of such encounters, is that sprawling mass of dense forest known to one and all as the Cannock Chase, which, as I have demonstrated is not at all far from the village of Woodseaves and the accursed Bridge 39.

For example, late one evening in early 1972, a man named Nigel Lea (no relation, so far as can be ascertained, to Rob Lea of 'Cult of the Moon Beast' infamy) was driving across the Cannock Chase, when his attention was suddenly drawn to a strange ball of glowing, blue light that slammed into the ground some distance ahead of his vehicle, and amid a veritable torrent of bright, fiery sparks. Needless to say, Lea quickly slowed his car down; and as he approached the approximate area where the light had fallen, was shocked and horrified to see looming before him, 'the biggest bloody dog I have ever seen in my life'.

Muscular and black, with large, pointed ears and huge paws, the creature seemed to positively ooze menace and negativity, and had a wild, staring look in its yellow-tinged eyes. For twenty or thirty seconds, both man and beast alike faced each other, after which time the 'animal' slowly and cautiously headed for the tall trees, never once taking its penetrating eyes off the petrified driver. Somewhat ominously, and around two or three weeks later, says Lea, a close friend of his was killed in an industrial accident under horrific circumstances; something which Lea believes – after having later deeply studied the history of Black Dog lore and its links with tragedy, death and the after-life – was directly connected with his strange encounter on that tree-shrouded Cannock Chase road back in 1972.

In the early to mid 1980s, noteworthy reports began to surface from the folk of the Cannock Chase of something that became known as the 'Ghost Dog of Brereton' – a reference to the specific locale from where most of the sightings originated. Yet again, the dog was described as being both large and menacing, and on at least two occasions it reportedly vanished into thin air after having been seen by terrified members of the public on lonely stretches of road late at night.

In direct response to an article that had appeared in the *Cannock Advertiser* newspaper during the winter of 1984/5 on the sightings of Brereton's infamous ghost dog, a member of the public from a local village wrote to the newspaper thus:

> `'On reading the article my husband and I were`
> `astonished. We recalled an incident which hap-`
> `pened in July some four or five years ago driv-`
> `ing home from a celebration meal at the Cedar`
> `Tree restaurant at about 11.30 p.m. We had`
> `driven up Coal Pit Lane and were just on the`
> `bends before the approach to the Holly Bush`
> `when, from the high hedge of trees on the right`
> `hand side of the road, the headlights picked`
> `out a misty shape which moved across the road`
> `and into the trees opposite.'`

The writer continued:

'We both saw it. It had no definite shape seeming to be a ribbon of mist about 18in. to 2ft. in depth and perhaps nine or 10ft. long with a definite beginning and end. It was a clear, warm night with no mist anywhere else. We were both rather stunned and my husband's first words were: "My goodness! Did you see that?" I remember remarking I thought it was a ghost. Until now we had no idea of the history of the area or any possible explanation for a haunting. Of course, this occurrence may be nothing to do with the "ghost dog" or may even have a natural explanation. However, we formed the immediate impression that what we saw was something paranormal.'

Possibly of relevance to the tale of the ghost dog of Brereton was the story of a man named Ivan Vinnel. In 1934, as a twelve-year-old, he had a strange encounter in his hometown of nearby Burntwood. The sun was setting and young Ivan and a friend were getting ready to head home after an afternoon of playing hide-and-seek. Suddenly, however, the pair was stopped dead in its tracks by the shocking sight of a ghostly 'tall, dark man', who was 'accompanied by a black dog' that had materialised out of a 'dense hedge' approximately ten yards from the boys' position. Both man and beast passed by in complete and utter silence before disappearing – quite literally.

Ivan later mentioned the incident to his uncle, who then proceeded to tell him that he, too, had seen the ghostly dog on several occasions as a child. It was always in the same location: on the old road that stretches from the village of Woodhouses to an area of Burntwood, near the town's hospital. As with the overwhelming majority of all black dog legends reported throughout the centuries and from across the length and breadth of the British Isles, this particular ghostly animal would always faithfully follow the same path and walk the same stretch of road before vanishing as mysteriously as it had first appeared.

So how are any of these accounts – as intriguing as they most certainly are - even remotely connected to the Man-Monkey and its wild exploits? Well, consider carefully the following:

(a) Ancient lore holds that the phantom black dogs had the ability to appear and vanish in the blink of an eye – as did the Man-Monkey;

(b) The ghostly dogs would almost unanimously frequent the

same locations time and again, and particularly old bridges, waterways, paths and crossroads – again, just like the Man-Monkey;

(c) The spectral hounds sometimes exhibited signs of outright hostility – something of which the Man-Monkey of 1879 was *most certainly* guilty.

And there is more, too. Perhaps the most famous of all of the phantom hounds of old England are those that are said to have frequented the ancient roads and pathways of Norfolk, Essex, Suffolk, and Sussex: namely Black Shuck, the Shug-Monkey, and the Shock. The Shuck and the Shock are classic black dogs; whereas, interestingly enough, the Shug Monkey is described as being a combination of spectral monkey and immense hound. Even the names have intriguing origins: while some researchers consider the possibility that all of the appellations had their origins in the word 'Shucky' – an ancient east-coast term meaning 'shaggy' – others suggest a far more sinister theory; namely that Shock, Shuck, and Shug are all based upon the Anglo-Saxon 'scucca', meaning *demon*; a most apt description, for sure.

More notable is the fact that in the case of Danny Thomas, the Man-Monkey-like beast that he was so in fear of and that he firmly believed was solely responsible for the Tay Bridge disaster of 1879 became known as the Shuggy – a name that *must surely* have had the same, obscure point of origin as that of the Shug Monkey and Black Shuck. Equally notable is the fact that the phantom black dog would often appear just before, or during, a thunder-storm; we might postulate, perhaps a thunder-storm not unlike that which led to large-scale tragedy and disaster at the Tay Bridge on that long-gone fateful and fatal night in December 1879.

And I cannot resist a discussion of something that had been brought to my attention in 2000 by Rob 'Cult of the Moon-Beast' Lea and that I have not revealed until now. I happened to mention to Rob as we chatted that in the late 1980s I had investigated a Man-Monkey like encounter at Shugborough Hall. Rob, who was well acquainted with the legends of phantom black dogs and the Shug Monkey, asked me: 'Have you ever thought that maybe the name of Shugborough Hall might have had something to do with it being the borough of the Shug?' I have to confess that I had not. And while historians would dispute Rob's theory, it was difficult not to at least muse and wonder upon his intriguing words.

And just to hammer home the connections even further, phantom black dogs have, on occasion, been interpreted as the souls of departed human beings returned to our plane of existence in the form of vile, nightmarish beasts. Bob Trubshaw notes: 'Newgate Gaol was the scene of a haunting by "a walking spirit in the likeness of a black dog"'.

So the story went, says Trubshaw, 'Luke Hutton, a criminal executed at York in the late 1590s, left behind an account of the phantom hound. Published as a pamphlet in 1612, *The Discovery of a London Monster, called the black dog of Newgate* suggested the dog was the ghost of a scholar imprisoned in Newgate who had been killed and eaten by starving inmates.'

Then there is the weird tale of William and David Sutor. The dark saga all began late one night in December 1728, when William, a Scottish farmer, was hard at work in his fields and heard an unearthly shriek that was accompanied by a brief glimpse of a large, dark-coloured dog. And on several more occasions in both 1729 and 1730, the dog returned, always seemingly intent on plaguing the Sutor family. However, it was in late November of 1730 that the affair ultimately reached its apex.

Once again the mysterious dog manifested before the farmer, but this time, incredibly, it was supposedly heard to speak, and uttered the following, concise words: 'Come to the spot of ground within half an hour.' The shocked William did so; and there waiting for him was the spectral hound. 'In the name of God and Jesus Christ, what are you that troubles me?' pleaded the terrified William. The hound answered that he was none other than David Sutor – William's brother - and that he had killed a man at that very spot some thirty-five years earlier.

William cried: 'David Sutor was a man and you appear as a dog.' To which the creature replied: 'I killed him with a dog; therefore I am made to appear as a dog, and I tell you to go bury these bones.' Finally on December 3, and after much frantic searching and digging, the bones of the man *were* finally found at the spot in question, and were given a respectful, Christian burial within the confines of the old Blair Churchyard. The dog – David Sutor in animalistic, spectral form – vanished, and was reportedly never seen again.

And on this latter theory - namely that some phantom beasts are the dead returned to walk the earth in a new, nightmarish guise - recall that Danny Thomas was a full-on believer that (a) the Shuggy of Scotland was his great-great grandfather, morphed into a hairy, hellish thing that had nothing but death and disaster upon its crazed and warped mind; and (b) that the chief sighting of the beast of Bridge 39 at Woodseaves occurred in the wake of the drowning of a man in the canal that sat deep below the infamous bridge.

Indeed, even the local police force had made the connection between the death of the man and the subsequent sightings of the hairy spectre.

But the final word on this matter I will leave, somewhat appropriately, with Charlotte Sophia Burne, who kicked off the whole controversy of the Man-Monkey in the pages of her book, *Shropshire Folklore*.

Commenting on the issue of 'the constant transformation of the departed into animals', Burne wrote in 1883 that: 'I believe this to have originated in the classical and medieval notion of werewolves, living men who could assume the shape of a wolf at pleasure. Sometimes also a corpse would arise from its grave in the form of a wolf, and might do incalculable damage if it were not at once beheaded and cast into the nearest stream.

'This is a Prussian fancy, and the English King John too is said to have gone about as a werewolf after his death. Wolves have been extinct in England long enough to have disappeared from popular tales though not so many centuries as most people suppose, but the Man-Monkey seems very like the old fable in a new guise.'

How curious that in 1883 Charlotte Sophia Burne should have made a connection between the Man-Monkey of Bridge 39 and old legends of werewolves, given the stories of Rob Lea and Simon that both delved into the world of the werewolf, too.

And now, with a veritable plethora of testimony and a variety of theories divulged, discussed and dissected, where does that leave us? Where else? The end, of course…

CONCLUSIONS

Twenty-one years have now flown by since I first immersed myself in the macabre and surreal realm of the Man-Monkey; and seven years have now passed since my studies came to a halt, several months before I moved to Texas to live. Yet, still the Man-Monkey continues to haunt me. Just occasionally, on those dark and stormy nights when the wind howls, the thunder booms, the lightning flashes, and the driving rain beats down on the windows of our Dallas flat (which, you may be intrigued to learn, is surprisingly regularly for a state renowned for its blisteringly hot temperatures), I find myself pondering and brooding upon those long-gone years and that vile, nightmarish creature.

Whether a purely physical animal (or animals), a Kelpie-type shape-shifting entity, a supernatural beast linked with the tales of the infernal Black Dogs of old England, a combination of all of the above, or something else entirely, I still know not. Definitive answers still frustratingly elude me, and quite possibly always will do so. I do know one thing for certain, however: that *something* haunts Bridge 39 near Woodseaves, and has done so for nigh-on 130 years - and possibly even longer, if the story of Florrie Abbott can be said to have some merit; which I most firmly believe it does.

Perhaps, after having now digested my words on the nature of the beast, you too will feel enthused and energised enough to launch your own investigation of the strange creature that lurks within the deep woods of the old Shropshire Union Canal. I wish you the very best of British luck. And, always remember: take great care and tread very carefully as you travel the tree-shrouded pathways of that cursed canal.

Something may *still* be watching, waiting, and poised to pounce…

ACKNOWLEDGEMENTS

I would like to offer my sincere thanks to the following people, without whom this book certainly could not have been written:

Everyone at the Devonshire-based Centre for Fortean Zoology, but particularly my good friend Jon Downes, for encouraging me to write this book, his lovely wife, Corinna, the ever-reliable Mark North, for the superb job he did on the layout and artwork, Graham Inglis and Richard Freeman, for laughs and insight into some of the strange and eccentric realms of cryptozoology; Mike Lockley, Editor of the *Chase Post* newspaper, for giving me the space to highlight the dark antics of the Man-Monkey; Simon, Gavin, Florrie Abbott, Bob Carroll, Norman Dodd, Danny Thomas, Peggy and Kathleen Baker, Rob Lea, Paul Bell, Mick Dodds, Mike Atkins and Nigel Lea, for their stories; Natalie Bhogal and all at http://www.waterscape.com for the use of material on the Man-Monkey and the Shropshire Union Canal from their website; my wife, Dana, who views my crypto-zoological pursuits and adventures with a mixture of amusement and bemusement; and my parents for taking me to Loch Ness on that long-gone holiday back in the summer of 1969.

CHRONOLOGY OF EVENTS

1848: In the 1920s, Florrie Abbott is told of an encounter with the Man-Monkey that reportedly occurred at the village of Ranton at some point in 1848.

*

January 1879: The Man-Monkey is seen at Bridge 39 on the Shropshire Union Canal. A distant relative of Danny Thomas commits suicide by jumping off Scotland's Tay Bridge.

*

December 1879: A wild, hairy man is seen atop the Tay Bridge shortly before it collapses, killing seventy-five people.

*

1883: *Shropshire Folklore*, by Charlotte S. Burne & Georgina F. Jackson, is published and tells the story of the January 1879 encounter with the Man-Monkey.

*

1910s: In 1995, researcher Rob Lea is told of a series of werewolf encounters near Bridge 39 at some point in the 1910s.

*

1940s: At the height of the Second World War and late at night, an upright bear-like beast is seen at the village of Woodseaves.

*

1960s: An employee of Shugborough Hall, Staffordshire, claims knowledge of an encounter that involves a large monkey-like creature on the grounds of the hall.

*

January or February of 1972 or 1973: Lorry-driver Bob Carroll becomes a personal witness to the activities of the Man-Monkey at Bridge 39.

*

Summer 1976: Paul Bell encounters both a hair-covered, upright animal and a large, eel-like creature on the Shropshire Union Canal.

*

1980: Janet and Colin Bord's book, *Alien Animals*, is published and resurrects the story of the Man-Monkey, as originally told to Charlotte S. Burne.

*

1981: Rumours circulate around the aforementioned Shugborough Hall that sightings of a large ape-like entity are linked with occult activities and practices, as well as with the strange deaths of a number of animals in the immediate area.

*

Summer 1982: Simon and a friend see the Man-Monkey at close-quarters on the stretch of canal near the village of Woodseaves.

*

1980s: According to information provided to the website waterscape. com, the Man-Monkey is seen by a witness while boating on the Shropshire Union Canal.

*

1986: Mick Dodds and his wife encounter a giant stag and are attacked by a marauding monkey near Chartley Castle, Staffordshire on the same day that the village of Abbots Bromley holds its historic Horn Dance.

*

1995: Jackie Houghton has a late-night encounter with a Bigfoot-style animal that she sees crossing the stretch of road that links the Staffordshire towns of Cannock and Rugeley.

*

1996: Mike Atkins sees a wild ape late at night near the Blithfield Reservoir.

*

1997: Gavin claims a close encounter with a hairy man-beast on the Cannock Chase.

*

Winter 1997: Peggy and Kathleen Baker see a large, hair-covered beast in the village of Ranton.

*

August 2000: My article *Man-Monkey and Big Cats* is published in the *Chase Post* on August 31, 2000.

*

Late 2002: My article on the Man-Monkey is published in the British *Express & Star* newspaper. Craig Blackmore and a friend narrowly avoid contact with a hairy creature that lunges at their car.

REFERENCES

The following sources were consulted during the course of writing this book:

Books:

The History, Gazetteer and Directory of Staffordshire, 1851

Shropshire Folklore, Charlotte S. Burne & Georgina F. Jackson, Trubner, 1883

The Legendary Lore of the Holy Wells of England, Including Rivers, Lakes, Fountains and Springs, Robert Charles Hope, Elliot Stock Books, 1893

Folklore, Myths and Legends of Britain, The Reader's Digest Association, Ltd, 1973

The Fate of the Dead, Theo Brown, Folklore Society Mistletoe Series, 1979

Alien Animals, Janet & Colin Bord, Granada, 1980

Devon Ghosts, Theo Brown, Jarrold, 1982

Family Holidays Around Dartmoor, Theo & Dorothy Brown, Devonshire Association for the Advancement of Science, 1995

The Mothman Prophecies, John Keel, Tor Books, 2001

The Strangest Pubs in Britain: Seeing is Believing, written and published by Strangest Books, 2002

Dark Dorset, Mark North & Robert Newland, Oakmagic Publications, 2002

Supernatural Dartmoor, Michael Williams, Bossiney Books, 2003

Monster Hunter, Jonathan Downes, CFZ Press, 2004

Three Men Seeking Monsters, Nick Redfern, Paraview-Pocket Books, 2004

Explore Phantom Black Dogs, Bob Trubshaw (Editor), Heart of Albion Press, 2005

The Owlman and Others, Jonathan Downes, CFZ Press, 2006

Monster! The A-Z of Zooform Phenomena, Neil Arnold, CFZ Press, 2007

Websites:

For more data on the history of Dundonald Castle, see: www. dundonaldcastle.org

For more data on British man-beasts, see: www.beastwatch.co.uk

For more data on Mark Fraser's Scottish Bigfoot reports, see: www. scottishbigcats.org

For more data on the Centre for Fortean Zoology, see: www.cfz.org. uk

For more data on Kelpies, see: www.mysteriousbritain.co.uk

For more data on Cannock Chase, see: www.cannock-chase.net

For more data on the Shropshire Union Canal, see: www.waterscape. com

For more data on the 1879 collapse of Scotland's Tay Bridge, see: www.taybridgedisaster.co.uk

For more data on Shugbrough Hall, Staffordshire, see: www. shugborough.org.uk

For more data on Chartley Castle, Staffordshire, see: www.castleuk. net

For more data on Monkey Island, see: www.monkeyisland.com

See also: www.berkshirehistory.com/castles/monkey_island.html

For more data on Monkey Marsh Lock, see: www.answers.com/ topic/monkey-marsh-lock

For more data on the Cannock Chase Bigfoot, see: www.gcbro.com

For more data on English mermaid legends, see: www.antipope.org

For more data on Ray Wallace and Bigfoot, see: www.lorencoleman.com/raymond_wallace_obituary.html

For more data on Jessie Roestenberg's UFO encounter at Ranton, Staffordshire in 1954, see: www.scientificexploration.org

For more data on myths and legends of Staffordshire and Shropshire, see: www.paranormaldatabase.com

For more data on BBC weatherman Ian Mccaskill's 2003 visit to Cannock Chase in search of the Chase Bigfoot, see: http://news.bbc.co.uk/1/shared/spl/hi/programmes/ morning_show/html/myths.stm

For more data on the Hairy Hands of Dartmoor, see: www. legendarydartmoor.co.uk

For more data on Martyn's Ape, see: www.darkdorset.co.uk

For more data on the Cider House at Defford, see: www.english-heritage.org

For more data on the Abbots Bromley Horn Dance, see:
www.abbotsbromley.com/horndance.htm
For more data on the big cat of Chillington Hall, see *Big Cat Territory in our Midst* at www.shropshirestar.com
For more data on Aqualate Mere, see:
www.english-nature.org.uk

Newspapers:

Did They See the 'Ghost Dog of Brereton?, Cannock Advertiser*, January 18, 1985
One Ghost and His Dog, Lichfield Post, February 2, 1995
Chase Beast's Getting Bolder, Chase Post, March 2, 2000
Man-Monkeys and Big Cats, Chase Post, August 31, 2000
Night Terror with a British Bigfoot, Express & Star, January 11, 2003
Where Did All the Doctor's Pets Go?, Chase Post, May 3, 2006

Magazines:

If You Go Down to the Woods Today, Jan Williams, *Animals & Men*, July 1994
Man Beasts and Beast Men, Jonathan Downes, *Encounters*, No. 3, 1996
The Werewolves of Britain, Nick Redfern, *Fate*, March 2006

Taken shortly after his life-changing visit to Loch Ness in the summer of 1969, a scowling and brooding 4-year-old Nick Redfern was already contemplating the monstrous mysteries of this world and beyond.

Nick Redfern

ABOUT THE AUTHOR

Born and raised in England and now residing in Dallas, Texas with his beloved wife, Dana, Nick Redfern developed a keen interest in all-things weird as a child. He is the author of many books on various aspects of Forteana, and he runs the American Office of the Centre for Fortean Zoology. For details, see his blog *There's Something in the Woods* at: http://monsterusa.blogspot.com

Nick's passions include Cryptozoology, UFOlogy, new-wave and punk-rock music, Carlsberg Special Brew Lager, ultra-violent zombie films, British chocolate, burnt toast covered with lashings of margarine, whisky-and-coke, chocolate milk-shakes, margaritas, and black t-shirts. He is a big fan of *Lovejoy, Jonathan Creek, The Midsomer Murders* and the published works of Jack Kerouac.

He has three heroes: Johnny Ramone (the late and lamented guitarist with the *Ramones*); Steve Jones of the *Sex Pistols* (who is neither late nor lamented); and long-dead British comedic character actor, Moore Marriott.

He can be contacted at his website: http://www.nickredfern.com

He can also be contacted at his additional blogs: http://www.ufomystic.com and http://nickcelebritysecrets.blogspot.com

THE CENTRE FOR FORTEAN ZOOLOGY

So, what is the Centre for Fortean Zoology?

We are a non profit-making organisation founded in 1992 with the aim of being a clearing house for information and coordinating research into mystery animals around the world. We also study out of place animals, rare and aberrant animal behaviour, and Zooform Phenomena; – little-understood "things" that appear to be animals, but which are in fact nothing of the sort, and not even alive (at least in the way we understand the term).

Why should I join the Centre for Fortean Zoology?

Not only are we the biggest organisation of our type in the world but - or so we like to think - we are the best. We are certainly the only truly *global* cryptozoological research organisation, and we carry out our investigations using a strictly scientific set of guidelines. We are expanding all the time and looking to recruit new members to help us in our research into mysterious animals and strange creatures across the globe. Why should you join us? Because, if you are genuinely interested in trying to solve the last great mysteries of Mother Nature, there is nobody better than us with whom to do it.

What do I get if I join the Centre for Fortean Zoology?

You get a four-issue subscription to our journal *Animals & Men*. Each issue contains 60 pages packed with news, articles, letters, research papers, field reports, and even a gossip column! The magazine is A5 in format with a full colour cover. You also have access to one of the world's largest collections of resource material dealing with cryptozoology and allied disciplines, and people from the CFZ membership regularly take part in fieldwork and expeditions around the world.

How is the Centre for Fortean Zoology organized?

The CFZ is managed by a three-man board of trustees, with a non-profit making trust registered with HM Government Stamp Office. The board of trustees is supported by a Permanent Directorate of full and part-time staff, and advised by a Consultancy Board of specialists - many of whom who are world-renowned experts in their particular field. We have regional representatives across the UK, the USA, and many other parts of the world, and are affiliated with other organisations whose aims and protocols mirror our own.

I am new to the subject, and although I am interested I have little practical knowledge. I don't want to feel out of my depth. What should I do?

Don't worry. We were *all* beginners once. You'll find that the people at the CFZ are friendly and approachable. We have a thriving forum on the website which is the hub of an ever-growing electronic community. You will soon find your feet. Many members of the CFZ Permanent Directorate started off as ordinary members, and now work full time chasing monsters around the world.

I have an idea for a project which isn't on your website. What do I do?

Write to us, e-mail us, or telephone us. The list of future projects on the website is not exhaustive. If you have a good idea for an investigation, please tell us. We may well be able to help.

How do I go on an expedition?

We are always looking for volunteers to join us. If you see a project that interests you, do not hesitate to get in touch with us. Under certain circumstances we can help provide funding for your trip. If you look on the future projects section of the website, you can see some of the projects that we have pencilled in for the next few years.

In 2003 and 2004 we sent three-man expeditions to Sumatra looking for Orang-Pendek - a semi-legendary bipedal ape. The same three went to Mongolia in 2005. All three members started off merely subscribers to the CFZ magazine.

Next time it could be you!

Project Kerinci, Sumatra - 2003
In search of the bipedal ape Orang Pendek

How is the Centre for Fortean Zoology funded?

We have no magic sources of income. All our funds come from donations, membership fees, works that we do for TV, radio or magazines, and sales of our publications and merchandise. We are always looking for corporate sponsorship, and other sources of revenue. If you have any ideas for fund-raising please let us know. However, unlike other cryptozoological organisations in the past, we do not live in an intellectual ivory tower. We are not afraid to get our hands dirty, and furthermore we are not one of those organisations where the membership have to raise money so that a privileged few can go on expensive foreign trips. Our research teams both in the UK and abroad, consist of a mixture of experienced and inexperienced personnel. We are truly a community, and work on the premise that the benefits of CFZ membership are open to all.

What do you do with the data you gather from your investigations and expeditions?

Reports of our investigations are published on our website as soon as they are available. Preliminary reports are posted within days of the project finishing.

We also publish a 200 page yearbook containing research papers and expedition reports too long to be printed in the journal. We freely circulate our information to anybody who asks for it.

No. Each year since 2000 we have held our annual convention - the *Weird Weekend* - in North Devon. It is three days of lectures, workshops, and excursions. But most importantly it is a chance for members of the CFZ to meet each other, and to talk with the members of the permanent directorate in a relaxed and informal setting and preferably with a pint of beer in one hand.

We are hoping to start up some regional groups in both the UK and the US which will have regular meetings, work together on research projects, and maybe have a mini convention of their own.

Since relocating to North Devon in 2005 we have become ever more closely involved with other community organisations, and we hope that this trend will continue. We also work closely with Police Forces across the UK as consultants for animal mutilation cases, and during 2006 we intend to forge closer links with the coastguard and other community services. We want to work closely with those who regularly travel into the Bristol Channel, so that if the recent trend of exotic animal visitors to our coastal waters continues, we can be out there as soon as possible.

Plans are also afoot to found a Visitor's Centre in rural North Devon. This will provide a museum, a library and an educational resource for our members and for researchers across the globe. We are also planning a youth organisation which will involve children and young people in our activities.

Apart from having been the only Fortean Zoological organisation in the world to have consistently published material on all aspects of the subject for over a decade, we have achieved impressive results, including:

- *Disproved the myth relating to the headless so-called sea-serpent carcass of Durgan beach in Cornwall 1975*

- *Disproved the story of the 1988 puma skull of Lustleigh Cleave*

- *Carried out the only in-depth research ever done into mythos of the Cornish Owlman*

- *Made the first records of a tropical species of lamprey*

- *Made the first records of a luminous cave gnat larva in Thailand.*

- *Discovered a possible new species of British mammal - The Beech Marten.*

- *In 1994-6 carried out the first archival fortean zoological survey of Hong Kong.*

- *In the year 2000, CFZ theories where confirmed when an entirely new species of lizard was found resident in Britain.*

- *Proved Existance of giant pike in Llangorse Lake*

- *Confirmed evidence of habitat increase of Armitage's Skink in The Gambia*

EXPEDITIONS & INVESTIGATIOINS TO DATE INCLUDE

- 1998 Puerto Rico, Florida, Mexico *(Chupacabras)*
- 1999 Nevada *(Bigfoot)*
- 2000 Thailand *(Giant Snakes called Nagas)*
- 2002 Martin Mere *(Giant catfish)*
- 2002 Cleveland *(Wallaby mutilation)*
- 2003 Bolam Lake *(BHM Reports)*
- 2003 Sumatra *(Orang Pendek)*
- 2003 Texas *(Bigfoot; Giant Snapping Turtles)*
- 2004 Sumatra *(Orang Pendek; Cigau, a Sabre-toothed cat)*
- 2004 Illinois *(Black Panthers; Cicada Swarm)*
- 2004 Texas *(Mystery Blue Dog)*
- 2004 Puerto Rico *(Chupacabras; carnivorous cave snails)*
- 2005 Belize *(Affiliate expedition for hairy dwarfs)*
- 2005 Mongolia *(Allghoi Khorkhoi aka Death Worm)*
- 2006 The Gambia *(Gambo - Gambian sea monster , Ninki Nanka and the Armitage's skink)*
- 2006 Llangorse Lake *(Giant Pike, Giant Eels)*
- 2006 Windermere *(Giant Eels)*

THE CENTRE FOR FORTEAN ZOOLOGY

www.cfz.org.uk

To apply for a <u>FREE</u> information pack about the organisation and details of how to join, plus information on current and future projects, expeditions and events.

Send a stamp addressed envelope to:

**THE CENTRE FOR FORTEAN ZOOLOGY
MYRTLE COTTAGE, WOOLSERY,
BIDEFORD, NORTH DEVON
EX39 5QR.**

or alternatively visit our website at:
w w w . c f z . o r g . u k

Other books available from
CFZ PRESS

CFZ PRESS

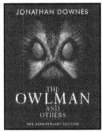

THE OWLMAN AND OTHERS - 30th Anniversary Edition
Jonathan Downes - ISBN 978-1-905723-02-7

£14.99

EASTER 1976 - Two young girls playing in the churchyard of Mawnan Old Church in southern Cornwall were frightened by what they described as a "nasty bird-man". These sightings have continued to the present day. These grotesque and frightening episodes have fascinated researchers for three decades now, and one man has spent years collecting all the available evidence into a book. To mark the 30th anniversary of these sightings, Jonathan Downes, has published a special edition of his book.

DRAGONS - More than a myth?
Richard Freeman - ISBN 0-9512872-9-X

£14.99

First scientific look at dragons since 1884. It looks at dragon legends worldwide, and examines modern sightings of dragon-like creatures, as well as some of the more esoteric theories surrounding dragonkind. Dragons are discussed from a folkloric, historical and cryptozoological perspective, and Richard Freeman concludes that: *"When your parents told you that dragons don't exist - they lied!"*

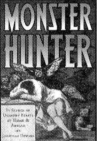

MONSTER HUNTER
Jonathan Downes - ISBN 0-9512872-7-3

£14.99

Jonathan Downes' long-awaited autobiography, *Monster Hunter*... Written with refreshing candour, it is the extraordinary story of an extraordinary life, in which the author crosses paths with wizards, rock stars, terrorists, and a bewildering array of mythical and not so mythical monsters, and still just about manages to emerge with his sanity intact.......

MONSTER OF THE MERE
Jonathan Downes - ISBN 0-9512872-2-2

£12.50

It all starts on Valentine's Day 2002, when a Lancashire newspaper announces that "Something" has been attacking swans at a nature reserve in Lancashire. Eyewitnesses have reported that a giant unknown creature has been dragging fully grown swans beneath the water at Martin Mere. An intrepid team from the Exeter based Centre for Fortean Zoology, led by the author, make two trips – each of a week – to the lake and its surrounding marshlands. During their investigations they uncover a thrilling and complex web of historical fact and fancy, quasi Fortean occurrences, strange animals and even human sacrifice.

**CFZ PRESS, MYRTLE COTTAGE,
WOOLFARDISWORTHY BIDEFORD,
NORTH DEVON, EX39 5QR
w w w . c f z . o r g . u k**

Other books available from
CFZ PRESS

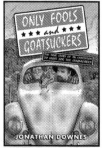

ONLY FOOLS AND GOATSUCKERS
Jonathan Downes - ISBN 0-9512872-3-0

£12.50

In January and February 1998 Jonathan Downes and Graham Inglis of the Centre for Fortean Zoology spent three and a half weeks in Puerto Rico, Mexico and Florida, accompanied by a film crew from UK Channel 4 TV. Their aim was to make a documentary about the terrifying chupacabra - a vampiric creature that exists somewhere in the grey area between folklore and reality. This remarkable book tells the gripping, sometimes scary, and often hilariously funny, story of how the boys from the CFZ did their best to subvert the medium of contemporary TV documentary making,and actually do their job.

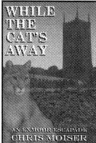

WHILE THE CAT'S AWAY
Chris Moiser - ISBN: 0-9512872-1-4

£7.99

Over the past thirty years or so, there have been numerous sightings of large exotic cats, including black leopards, pumas and lynx, in the South West of England. Former Rhodesian soldier Sam McCall moved to North Devon and became a farmer and pub owner when Rhodesia became Zimbabwe in 1980. Over the years despite many of his pub regulars having seen the "Beast of Exmoor" Sam wasn't at all sure that it existed. Then a series of happenings made him change his mind. Chris Moiser - a zoologist - is well known for his research into the mystery cats of the westcountry. This is his first novel.

CFZ EXPEDITION REPORT 2006 - GAMBIA
ISBN 1905723032

£12.50

In July 2006, The J.T.Downes memorial Gambia Expedition - a six-person team - Chris Moiser, Richard Freeman, Chris Clarke, Oll Lewis, Lisa Dowley and Suzi Marsh went to the Gambia, West Africa. They went in search of a dragon-like creature, known to the natives as `Ninki Nanka`, which has terrorized the tiny African state for generations, and has reportedly killed people as recently as the 1990s. They also went to dig up part of a beach where an amateur naturalist claims to have buried the carcass of a mysterious fifteen foot sea monster named 'Gambo', and they sought to find the Armitage's Skink (Chalcides armitagei) - a tiny lizard first described in 1922 and only rediscovered in 1989. Here, for the first time, is their story.... With an foreword by Dr. Karl Shuker and introduction by Jonathan Downes.

BIG CATS IN BRITAIN YEARBOOK 2006
Edited by Mark Fraser - ISBN 978-1905723-01-0

£10.00

Big cats are said to roam the British Isles and Ireland even now, as you are sitting and reading this. People from all walks of life encounter these mysterious felines on a daily basis, in every nook and cranny of these two countries. Most are jet-black, some are white, some are brown; in fact big cats of every description and colour are seen by some unsuspecting person while on his or her daily business. 'Big Cats in Britain' are the largest and most active research group in the British Isles and Ireland This is their first book. It contains a run-down of every known big cat sighting in the UK during 2005, together with essays by various luminaries of the British big cat research community which place the phenomenon into scientific, cultural, and historical perspective.

CFZ PRESS, MYRTLE COTTAGE,
WOOLFARDISWORTHY BIDEFORD,
NORTH DEVON, EX39 5QR
w w w . c f z . o r g . u k

Other books available from
CFZ PRESS

CFZ PRESS

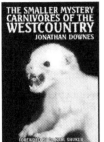

THE SMALLER MYSTERY CARNIVORES OF THE WESTCOUNTRY
Jonathan Downes - ISBN 978-1-905723-05-8

£7.99

Although much has been written in recent years about the mystery big cats which have been reported stalking Westcountry moorlands, little has been written on the subject of the smaller British mystery carnivores. This unique book redresses the balance and examines the current status in the Westcountry of three species thought to be extinct: the Wildcat, the Pine Marten, and the Polecat, finding that the truth is far more exciting than the currently held scientific dogma. This book also uncovers evidence suggesting that even more exotic species of small mammal may lurk hitherto unsuspected in the countryside of Devon, Cornwall, Somerset and Dorset.

THE BLACKDOWN MYSTERY
Jonathan Downes - ISBN 978-1-905723-00-3

£7.99

This is the soft underbelly of ufology, rife with unsavoury characters, plenty of drugs and booze." That sums it up quite well, we think. A new edition of the classic 1999 book by legendary fortean author Jonathan Downes.

In this remarkable book, Jon weaves a complex tale of conspiracy, anti-conspiracy, quasi-conspiracy and downright lies surrounding an air-crash and alleged UFO incident in Somerset during 1996. However the story is much stranger than that. This excellent and amusing book lifts the lid off much of contemporary forteana and explains far more than it initially promises.

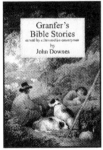

GRANFER'S BIBLE STORIES
John Downes - ISBN 0-9512872-8-1

£7.99

Bible stories in the Devonshire vernacular, each story being told by an old Devon Grandfather - 'Granfer'. These stories are now collected together in a remarkable book presenting selected parts of the Bible as one more-or-less continuous tale in short 'bite sized' stories intended for dipping into or even for bed-time reading. `Granfer` treats the biblical characters as if they were simple country folk living in the next village. Many of the stories are treated with a degree of bucolic humour and kindly irreverence, which not only gives the reader an opportunity to re-evaluate familiar tales in a new light, but do so in both an entertaining and a spiritually uplifting manner.

FRAGRANT HARBOURS DISTANT RIVERS
John Downes - ISBN 0-9512872-5-7

£12.50

Many excellent books have been written about Africa during the second half of the 19th Century, but this one is unique in that it presents the stories of a dozen different people, whose interlinked lives and achievements have as many nuances as any contemporary soap opera. It explains how the events in China and Hong Kong which surrounded the Opium Wars, intimately effected the events in Africa which take up the majority of this book. The author served in the Colonial Service in Nigeria and Hong Kong, during which he found himself following in the footsteps of one of the main characters in this book, Frederick Lugard – the architect of modern Nigeria.

CFZ PRESS, MYRTLE COTTAGE, WOOLFARDISWORTHY BIDEFORD, NORTH DEVON, EX39 5QR
w w w . c f z . o r g . u k

CFZ PRESS

Other books available from
CFZ PRESS

ANIMALS & MEN - Issues 1 - 5 - In the Beginning
Edited by Jonathan Downes - ISBN 0-9512872-6-5

£12.50

At the beginning of the 21st Century monsters still roam the remote, and sometimes not so remote, corners of our planet. It is our job to search for them. The
Centre for Fortean Zoology [CFZ] is the only professional, scientific and full-time
organisation in the world dedicated to cryptozoology - the study of unknown animals. Since 1992 the CFZ has carried out an unparalleled programme of research
and investigation all over the world. We have carried out expeditions to Sumatra
(2003 and 2004), Mongolia (2005), Puerto Rico (1998 and 2004), Mexico (1998),
Thailand (2000), Florida (1998), Nevada (1999 and 2003), Texas (2003 and 2004),
and Illinois (2004). An introductory essay by Jonathan Downes, notes putting each
issue into a historical perspective, and a history of the CFZ.

ANIMALS & MEN - Issues 6 - 10 - The Number of the Beast
Edited by Jonathan Downes - ISBN 978-1-905723-06-5

£12.50

At the beginning of the 21st Century monsters still roam the remote, and sometimes
not so remote, corners of our planet. It is our job to search for them. The Centre for
Fortean Zoology [CFZ] is the only professional, scientific and full-time organisation
in the world dedicated to cryptozoology - the study of unknown animals. Since 1992
the CFZ has carried out an unparalleled programme of research and investigation
all over the world. We have carried out expeditions to Sumatra (2003 and 2004),
Mongolia (2005), Puerto Rico (1998 and 2004), Mexico (1998), Thailand (2000), Florida (1998), Nevada (1999 and 2003), Texas (2003 and 2004), and Illinois (2004).
Preface by Mark North and an introductory essay by Jonathan Downes, notes putting each issue into a historical perspective, and a history of the CFZ.

BIG BIRD! Modern Sightings of Flying Monsters

£7.99

Ken Gerhard - ISBN 978-1-905723-08-9

Today, from all over the dusty U.S. / Mexican border, come hair-raising stories of modern day encounters with winged monsters of immense size and terrifying appearance. Further field sightings of
similar creatures are recorded from all around the globe: The Kongamato of Africa, the Ropen of New
Guinea and many others. What lies behind these weird tales? Ken Gerhard is in pole position to find
out. A native Texan, he lives in the homeland of the monster some call 'Big Bird'. Cryptozoologist,
author, adventurer, and gothic musician, Ken is a larger than life character as amazing as the Big
Bird itself. Ken's scholarly work is the first of its kind. The research and fieldwork involved are indeed
impressive. On the track of the monster, Ken uncovers cases of animal mutilations, attacks on hu-
mans, and mounting evidence of a stunning zoological discovery ignored by mainstream science.
Something incredible awaits us on the broad desert horizon. Keep watching the skies!

STRENGTH THROUGH KOI
They saved Hitler's Koi and other stories

£7.99

Jonathan Downes - ISBN 978-1-905723-04-1

Strength through Koi is a book of short stories - some of them true,
some of them less so - by noted cryptozoologist and raconteur Jonathan
Downes. Very funny in parts, this book is highly recommended for anyone with even a passing interest in aquaculture.

CFZ PRESS, MYRTLE COTTAGE,
WOOLFARDISWORTHY BIDEFORD,
NORTH DEVON, EX39 5QR
w w w . c f z . o r g . u k

CFZ PRESS

Other books available from

BIG CATS IN BRITAIN YEARBOOK 2007
Edited by Mark Fraser - ISBN 978-1-905723-09-6

£12.50

Big cats are said to roam the British Isles and Ireland even now as you are sitting and reading this. People from all walks of life encounter these mysterious felines on a daily basis in every nook and cranny of these two countries. Most are jet-black, some are white, some are brown, in fact big cats of every description and colour are seen by some unsuspecting person while on his or her daily business. 'Big Cats in Britain' are the largest and most active group in the British Isles and Ireland This is their first book. It contains a run-down of every known big cat sighting in the UK during 2006, together with essays by various luminaries of the British big cat research community which place the phenomenon into scientific, cultural, and historical perspective.

CAT FLAPS! Northern Mystery Cats
Andy Roberts - ISBN 978-1-905723-11-9

£6.99

Of all Britain's mystery beasts, the alien big cats are the most renowned. In recent years the notoriety of these uncatchable, out-of-place predators have eclipsed even the Loch Ness Monster. They slink from the shadows to terrorise a community, and then, as often as not, vanish like ghosts. But now film, photographs, livestock kills, and paw prints show that we can no longer deny the existence of these once-legendary beasts. Here then is a case-study, a true lost classic of Fortean research by one of the country's most respected researchers; Andy Roberts. Cat Flaps! is the product of many years of research and field work in the 1970s and 80s, an odyssey through the phantom felids of the North East of England. Follow Andy on his flat cap safari as he trails such creatures as the 'Whitby lynx', the 'Harrogate panther', and the 'Durham puma'. Written with humour, intelligence, and a healthy dose of scepticism, Cat Flaps! is a book that deserves a place on the bookshelf of every cryptozoologist.

CENTRE FOR FORTEAN ZOOLOGY 2007 YEARBOOK
Edited by Jonathan Downes and Richard Freeman
ISBN 978-1-905723-14-0

£12.50

The Centre For Fortean Zoology Yearbook is a collection of papers and essays too long and detailed for publication in the CFZ Journal Animals & Men. With contributions from both well-known researchers, and relative newcomers to the field, the Yearbook provides a forum where new theories can be expounded, and work on little-known cryptids discussed.

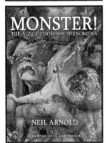

MONSTER! THE A-Z OF ZOOFORM PHENOMENA
Neil Arnold
ISBN 978-1-905723-10-2

£14.99

Zooform Phenomena are the most elusive, and least understood, mystery `animals`. Indeed, they are not animals at all, and are not even animate in the accepted terms of the word, but entities or apparitions which adopt, or seem to have (quasi) animal form.

These arcane and contentious entities have plagued cryptozoology - the study of unknown animals - since its inception, and tend to be dismissed by mainstream science as thoroughly unworthy of consideration. But they continue to be seen, and Jonathan Downes - the Director of the Centre for Fortean Zoology - who first coined the term in 1990, maintains that many zooforms result from a synergy of complex psychosocial and sociological issues, and suggests that to classify all such phenomena as "paranormal" in origin is counterproductive, and for researchers to dismiss them out of hand is thoroughly unscientific.

Author and researcher Neil Arnold is to be commended for a groundbreaking piece of work, and has provided the world's first alphabetical listing of zooforms from around the world.

CFZ PRESS, MYRTLE COTTAGE, WOOLFARDISWORTHY BIDEFORD, NORTH DEVON, EX39 5QR
w w w . c f z . o r g . u k

Other books available from
CFZ PRESS

BIG CATS LOOSE IN BRITAIN
Marcus Matthews - ISBN 978-1-905723-12-6

£14.99

Big Cats: Loose in Britain, looks at the body of anecdotal evidence for such creatures: sightings, livestock kills, pawprints and photographs, and seeks to determine underlying commonalities and threads of evidence. These two strands are repeatedly woven together into a highly readable, yet scientifically compelling overview of the big cat phenomenon in Britain.

DARK DORSET
TALES OF MYSTERY, WONDER AND TERROR
Robert. J. Newland and Mark. J. North
ISBN 978-1-905723-15-6

£12.50

This extensively illustrated compendium has over 400 tales and references making this book by far one of the best in its field. Dark Dorset has been thoroughly researched, and includes many new entries and up to date information never before published. The title of the book speaks for its self, and is indeed not for the faint hearted or those easily shocked.

CFZ PRESS, MYRTLE COTTAGE, WOOLFARDISWORTHY BIDEFORD, NORTH DEVON, EX39 5QR
www.cfz.org.uk

Lightning Source UK Ltd.
Milton Keynes UK
UKHW022007141122
412192UK00007B/790